P9-CRL-636

★ GAME FOR LIFE ★

JOHN MADDEN

A PRO FOOTBALL HALL OF FAME BIOGRAPHY

★ GAME FOR LIFE BIOGRAPHIES ★

John Madden

Michael Strahan

Troy Aikman

★ GAME FOR LIFE ★

JOHN MADDEN

A PRO FOOTBALL HALL OF FAME BIOGRAPHY

Peter Richmond

RANDOM HOUSE
NEW YORK

Copyright © 2019 by Pro Football Hall of Fame

All rights reserved. Published in the United States by
Random House Children's Books, a division of
Penguin Random House LLC, New York.

Random House and the colophon are registered
trademarks of Penguin Random House LLC.

Visit us on the Web! rhcbooks.com

Educators and librarians, for a variety of teaching tools,
visit us at RHTeachersLibrarians.com

Library of Congress Cataloging-in-Publication Data
Name: Richmond, Peter, author.
Title: Game for life: John Madden / Peter Richmond.
Description: First edition. |
New York: Random House Children's Books, [2019]
Identifiers: LCCN 2018029166 | ISBN 978-1-63565-246-8 (hardcover) |
ISBN 978-1-63565-247-5 (ebook) | ISBN 978-1-9848-5211-3
(hardcover library binding)
Subjects: LCSH: Madden, John, 1936– —Juvenile literature. |
Football coaches—United States—Biography—Juvenile
literature. | Sportscasters—United States—Biography—
Juvenile literature.
Classification: LCC GV939.M28 R53 2019 | DDC 796.332092 [B]—dc23

Printed in the United States of America
10 9 8 7 6 5 4 3 2 1
First Edition

Random House Children's Books supports the First Amendment
and celebrates the right to read.

"Individual commitment to a group effort—that is what makes a team work, a company work, a society work, a civilization work."

—Vince Lombardi

CHAPTER 1

IT'S NOT EVERY KID who has a playing field named after him. Then again, it's not every kid who loves sports so much that he'd jump onto a moving freight train to get up to San Francisco to see his beloved San Francisco 49ers play. Or hitchhike to their training camp. Or hop a moving streetcar to catch a San Francisco Seals baseball game.

It's not everyone who loves sports so much that his whole world revolved around them when he was a kid.

And a teenager. And even now, as an adult.

It's not every guy who's been lucky enough to keep playing his whole life.

But John Madden has.

1

★ ★ ★

He was born in 1936 in Austin, Minnesota. When Madden was a young boy, his family moved to Daly City, California, where his father, an auto mechanic, got work at a Chevrolet dealership. Daly City was an industrial town—and a great place for a sports-loving kid to grow up in. It lay just south of San Francisco, home to the National Football League's 49ers and the Pacific Coast League's Seals.

Better yet, it was a town with a large municipal park full of ball fields, although the truth was that Madden and his friends spent most of their time in the humble patch of ground next to his family's home on Knowles Street.

The kids called it Madden's Lot—as in, "We'll meet after school at Madden's Lot."

"I thought it was my lot," Madden said. "I really did. You didn't know who owned things in those days. I thought *I* owned it. It's there, you play."

It wasn't much of a field: packed dirt, maybe sixty feet wide, a hundred feet long, not a lot of grass.

"It was a terrible lot," his lifelong friend John

Robinson said. "It was all weeds. Every time I go to a restaurant now and I see *Field Greens* as an expensive salad on the menu, I think of being tackled facedown with a mouthful of field greens as a kid."

Madden's Lot sloped a little downward. If you and your friends were playing football, and your side had the ball, and you were pretending to be, say, 49ers star running back Hugh McElhenny, the best play would be going downhill on a power sweep to the right.

For baseball, home plate was on the low side, and if you were Seals outfielder Neill Sheridan, your hit could clear Knowles Street. But if you pulled it too far left, you'd hit the Madden house.

"We'd break windows all the time, the dining room and kitchen," Madden said. "But my mom didn't say a word. My dad never said a word, either. That was a gift. I was lucky. It was never, 'You can't play anymore; don't break the window anymore.' He'd just fix it.

"Then he finally put chicken wire on the windows. I mean, he knew I couldn't tell my buddies,

'Let's play in Madden's Lot, but you can't break a window.'"

★ ★ ★

Daly City had one cool thing going for it that a lot of cities don't: it was right on the ocean. You could smell the sea, especially when the fog rolled in.

"Daly City was the fog capital of the world," Madden said. At least that's what it felt like to the young boy. "I grew up in fog. I love fog. You know why? You never get tired in fog. You can play all day. We'd play early in the morning before school, then it'd burn off, then after school, it came back, and you could play in the fog again. . . . The fog was great for endurance."

The science behind Madden's fog theory might be a little suspect, but whatever the reason, it seemed as if he could play his sports forever. This meant, of course, that being a kid was *not* about grammar school at Our Lady of Perpetual Help, where Madden was never a top student. "I always made fun of the people who sat in front, the people who, when

4

the nuns would ask a question, they'd be waving their hands.

"I never waved my hand. I just sat in back and talked about other stuff until I got in trouble, yeah. You'd go to the principal's office and *whack!*"

Grade school was about waiting: for recess, so he could play; for lunch, so he could play; and for the final bell, so he could play.

"If it was football season, we were Forty-Niners," Robinson said. "If it was baseball, we were Yankees. Basically, when we were little kids, you'd start playing at nine in the morning and go home either when the sun went down or you got so hungry you couldn't stand it anymore."

★ ★ ★

Daly City kids never had any money, and if you hustled enough to get a nickel or a dime, picking up balls at the end of a long day at Marchbank Park in Daly City, it'd usually go to a candy bar or ice cream. When you finally put together enough pennies to get that cone, it was a prize so special that you had to remember to say "No bites" when you got it, because if another kid said "Bites," you'd have to give him one.

Madden had a way around the "Bites" rule, by the way. If he forgot to say "No bites" and another kid yelled "Bites," Madden would spit in the ice cream. Of course, that didn't stop his friend John Robinson. John would eat the ice cream anyway.

That was when it was sort of decided they'd become lifelong buddies, playing sports and watching sports. For free. It was easy to sneak into old Kezar Stadium, at the southeast corner of Golden Gate Park, the 49ers' home back then. "You just got there real early," Madden said, "and walked in through an open gate."

"Two and a half hours early," Robinson said. "Sometimes you could pick up a buck selling seat cushions."

During baseball season, Madden's attention turned to the Seals of the Pacific Coast League, who played at Seals Stadium, over on Sixteenth and Bryant.

Back then, only sixteen teams were in Major League Baseball, so the level of play in the three

AAA leagues was high. The best Seals players might play in Yankee Stadium the next season. (Joe DiMaggio? Mr. Yankee? Whose fifty-six-game hitting streak set the major-league record? He had a sixty-one-game streak with the Seals.)

The team had an added attraction: the legendary Lefty O'Doul was the manager. Lefty had played for the Seals and then gone on to a Hall of Fame career in the majors. (In his best year, he hit .398, collected 32 home runs, and drove in 122 runs.)

It was Madden's first paying job that led to one of his first dreams coming true. He'd begun to earn a little money as a golf caddy. He made $1.50 for each round!

O'Doul would often play a round of golf before Sunday afternoon games, pulling into the parking lot of the club in his red Cadillac convertible. One day, he stuck his head into the caddy shack: "Anyone want to go to the game?"

Madden jumped up first. His friend Danny Rasmussen was next. Madden made Danny sit in the back.

Now, in 1948, there weren't any freeways, so

O'Doul had to drive through town: down Mission to Sixteenth, then up to Bryant Street. "I'm just hoping I run into someone I know so I can wave to them. 'There's John Madden riding with Lefty O'Doul in a Cadillac!' Of course, I didn't see a single guy I knew."

★ ★ ★

But playing the games beat watching them any day of the week, even if it meant getting into a pickup tackle game down at Marchbank Park with guys who were five years older. "You'd have to just suck it up when you got hit," Robinson said. "That was important. It was an important lesson to learn."

After grade school, Robinson went on to another Catholic school. Madden didn't even think about where he was going until he was actually there. "I didn't even think I was going to high school until I went to high school," Madden said. "I didn't think I was going to go to college until I went to college.

"It was just always, 'Where you going to play next year?'"

It turned out to be Jefferson High in Daly City. It was a higher level of education, but Madden's priorities didn't change. He kept playing, and every day of the school year revolved around football (he played on the offensive line), and baseball (he was a catcher), and basketball, his third sport. According to his pal Robinson, "He was a reasonable basketball player." Not exactly the highest praise. Madden generally stayed in the low post and looked for rebounds.

And even though football would turn out to be his passion, the young Madden was good enough as a catcher to attract the notice of major-league baseball scouts. He had a strong arm, and both the Boston Red Sox and the New York Yankees were interested in signing him.

Robinson was no slouch as a catcher, either, starting for his parochial high school team.

"Yeah, he had a great arm," Robinson said. "But one day in high school, I watched him do something no one has ever done. He threw a home run."

What?

"There were two out and two strikes, and then the guy struck out, but John dropped the ball. The guy starts running, and John stands up. He waits a second, because he has a powerful arm, and then he fires it to first—about fourteen feet too high. So now the ball stays fair and starts rolling out in right field. There's no fence, and the ball keeps rolling and rolling and rolling. The right fielder can't catch up to it. The guy goes all the way around and scores.

"'John,' I yelled, 'you threw a home run!' He wasn't real happy about it. It lost them the game. But no one else has ever thrown a home run, as far as I know."

Madden passed on the baseball offers to concentrate on football. He loved eating and now, in his late teens, was growing larger, particularly in his legs. "There comes a point in life when you grow out of one position and then grow into another position," he said. He was going to be an offensive lineman from then on.

By the last years of high school, Robinson and

Madden and their group of pals were spending their out-of-school time on more than sports. When Madden's dad gave him a car—"It was a big Cadillac, prewar, maybe '40. We called it the Hulk," Robinson said—everyone had to chip in for gas. "I'd go around feeling under the cushions on the couch looking for change to pay my share."

The destination? Sometimes it was the drive-in. One kid would drive in and pay, and everyone else would sneak in over the fence. But wherever they'd go, one thing was certain: the gang stayed together. You didn't go anywhere until you called up everyone.

In this group, you didn't put on airs. You didn't dress in fancy clothes. You didn't have much money, but that didn't matter. You had a whole lot of fun in the gang, where Madden and Robinson were the unspoken leaders.

Their friendship, thanks to a love of sports, is still as strong today as it was back then. One of them won a Super Bowl, retired with the best winning percentage of any pro football coach with at least one hundred games, and was inducted into the Pro Football Hall of Fame. The other coached USC to four Rose Bowl victories and the Los Angeles Rams to the playoffs six times.

Maybe their friendship lasted because two smart sports guys were always talking about sports, and making each other better coaches.

Or maybe it was the magic of the Daly City fog.

CHAPTER 2

BY NOW, WITH HIS athletic ability attracting notice, Madden started thinking about going to college. For one thing, he'd started caddying at the prestigious San Francisco Golf Club in high school and noticed that all the members of this club, the rich guys, had college degrees.

For another, working a different job in Redwood City at night, he'd taken to spending his days in the courtroom at the Redwood City Courthouse. Now he began to think about being a lawyer.

"I loved watching trials, because one side always wins," he said. "That's exactly what I wanted. To watch a trial. I always thought that the guy who was talking was winning. I kept swaying back and forth with each guy's argument. I was serious. I wanted to be a trial lawyer."

So now it was time to look for a scholarship. While his buddy Robinson went on to the high-profile program up the coast at the University of Oregon, Madden started out at College of San Mateo, fifteen miles down the road from Daly City.

He played football for one semester, on what he calls "an average team," before following Robinson up to the big time.

He enrolled at Oregon the following autumn. But the mechanic's kid and the upper-class football school were not a good fit. It wasn't just because some of the top teams in the University Division, now known as Division I, were adopting more wide-open offenses that didn't rely on bulky offensive linemen like Madden.

There were two other things he didn't like about Eugene, Oregon: rain and fraternities. Fog was fine. Rain wasn't.

As for the frat life, Madden has never liked to talk much about his experience in the land of the

Ducks. Fraternities are selective, often considering themselves clubs for special students, but everything about the down-to-earth Madden was the opposite of that. It wasn't going to work. Madden was already a man of the masses.

"Maybe you should take a little time off, play football at a different level," he was told—a very different level. Grays Harbor College in the seaside fishing town of Aberdeen, Washington, was a step down in football.

But it was a great place for life lessons. His off-the-field job involved sweeping up the back room at a local bar called the Mint Café. That's where the poker was played.

Madden's lifetime love of small-town America, and its people, was born at Grays Harbor. He'd been a talkative kid from early childhood on. He loved nothing more than meeting new people and learning new things.

But after one season of playing football for Grays Harbor, the question of "Where am I going to play next?" came up. That meant "playing baseball," because even if he wasn't going to be a pro baseball player, Madden couldn't let a baseball season go by without playing the game. Not the guy who lived to play.

And since colleges in Washington weren't well known for baseball, now it was back south—this time to California Polytechnic State University. Cal Poly–San Luis Obispo, as it's known, was a strong academic school and had competitive teams in the NCAA's College Division (later to become Division II)—including a powerful football team in the Big Sky Conference. He enrolled as a junior.

He and his roommate were a high-powered pair entering that year as football players. . . . But they started their careers at the bottom—literally.

"They put us in a room without windows under the stadium," said Bobby Beathard, a quarterback who would go on to a distinguished career as a football executive. As personnel director, he laid the foundation of the Super Bowl–winning Miami Dolphins. Later, as general manager, he helped guide the Washington Redskins to two Super Bowl victories and the San Diego Chargers to a Super Bowl appearance.

But that first semester? Exiled to a room the size of a closet? "It was like being in the military," Beathard said.

At least they didn't have far to go for practice. The field was about a hundred feet away.

Madden and Beathard took the same classes, and they found out that both of them were back-row guys.

"We were afraid if we sat up too close, we'd be called on," Beathard said.

Beathard still doesn't know why they were stuck in a tiny room where they had to use the stadium bathrooms while the rest of the team stayed in dorms. Maybe it made them more dedicated as team players. It definitely built a bond between the quarterback and his roommate, who was now a right tackle.

Beathard knew he could count on Madden. He also found out that his friend was a lot more athletic than the typical offensive lineman.

"He was one of the fastest guys on the team," Beathard remembered. "Tall and big and fast. When we ran sprints after practice, he was as fast as the wide receivers and defensive backs. He was also really smart, even though he wouldn't admit it. He was a student of the game."

As for being an ace student in the classroom? Not so much. That would change in a few years. For the time being, he was making his impression on the field. The team lost a total of five games in Beathard's three years, with Madden anchoring the line in front of him for two.

CHAPTER 3

EVEN THOUGH HE HAD a great first season at Cal Poly, Madden didn't expect to read what he read on the sports page of the newspaper shortly after the season's end. Before the NFL Draft became a big event, draft choices were only listed on the statistics page of the paper.

And there it was: *In Round 21, the Philadelphia Eagles take John Madden of Cal Poly-San Luis Obispo.* He'd been chosen to play in the NFL. But he was hardly excited: since he was a junior, he couldn't play for another year.

One year later, he made it to the academic finish line. (Beathard has proof. Hanging on a wall in his home in Tennessee is a framed photograph of him posing on graduation day with Madden.)

Then it was time to fly to training camp in Hershey, Pennsylvania. It seemed that the fabled career he'd only dreamed about had finally started. But in a cruel twist of fate, it ended before he could play in a single exhibition game. Before he could ever pull on his new green-and-white number seventy-seven in front of a roaring crowd.

The only witnesses to the play that ended his playing career were teammates and coaches. It was a routine goal-line running play.

"I was a guard on the left side," he said. "The pile came up behind me and rolled over on my leg."

Linemen didn't weigh three hundred pounds back then, but they were heavy enough for this pileup to cause a stab of hurt in Madden's left knee. Back then, the medical side of the game was pretty basic: you get hurt, you tape it up, and you get back out there. This hurt a little too much to keep playing, though, so Madden just limped to the locker room. There'd be no stretcher or cart. No way he'd let that happen.

But in the locker room, the team physician told

him he hadn't just torn some cartilage. He'd torn ligaments. His next stop would be the hospital for an operation.

After the operation, he found out that his season was over. He could play next year . . . maybe. But not likely. "What I had with my knee in those days, no one played again."

The worst thing about being laid up in the hospital for a couple of weeks? Not being able to go down to Philadelphia with his new team when the Eagles broke camp. After all, part of the fun of playing is playing with your teammates. "Being by yourself when the team wasn't there was tough."

What would Madden's future have been if he hadn't wrecked his knee that day? Maybe he would have been a starting offensive tackle. Maybe not. Maybe he would have hung in for a good career, then started at the bottom level of coaching, where he'd have had to learn the job, year by year. Maybe years down the road he'd have been considered for a head coaching job.

Instead, a few weeks after his operation, he started learning how to coach from a master.

The Eagles kept him on the payroll, and he stayed

in Philadelphia to rehabilitate the knee as best he could. He spent a lot of time in the training room in old Franklin Field, the Eagles' stadium, a horseshoe that was built (at first out of wood) thirty years after the end of the war—the *Civil* War (1895).

That meant showing up early in the morning to put his leg in the whirlpool tub before the team arrived and needed it. Only one other person was there each morning. But not just any person. The injured rookie had just lucked into a master class in football strategy, with a man who led the NFL in passing three different years and would become the only quarterback to beat Vince Lombardi's Green Bay Packers in a title game.

★ ★ ★

On his football card, it said *Norm Van Brocklin,* but to players, announcers, sportswriters, and fans alike, he was "the Dutchman." In the mid- to late fifties, when the NFL was first becoming popular with sports fans, the quarterbacks were the stars, and none was as charismatic as Van Brocklin.

A native of a tiny town in South Dakota, he'd left high school after his junior year to serve three years in the navy during World War II. He came back to play for the Los Angeles Rams, where he split quarterbacking duties with Bob Waterfield.

In 1951, his third year, he set a record for passing yardage in a single game that still stands—554. The Rams won the title that year in the Los Angeles Memorial Coliseum.

After losing the title game to the Cleveland Browns on a night when he threw six interceptions, the Dutchman decided to retire. He planned to get into business . . . until Eagles coach Buck Shaw told him that if he'd agree to a trade to Philadelphia, Van Brocklin would have total control of the offense.

He wasn't going to waste that opportunity. That's why, on those early mornings in the locker room, Madden had company. After Madden tried to rehab that knee, he'd go into the locker room and sit on the bench in front of his locker. Van Brocklin would be sitting next to a projector, studying film projected on a wall near the front of the locker room.

Van Brocklin never said anything at first, until one day he looked over his shoulder and said, "Hey, Red, come on up."

"So I went up and sat next to him," Madden said. "Now, I'm not saying I had any input. I just sat there and listened to him as he broke the film down. He'd just talk out loud: 'Geez, I think I can get that post. If I put Clarence Peaks out in the flat, I can get Tommy McDonald open. . . .' And I'm watching and seeing how he's thinking and you get ready to attack a defense. That's where I learned pro football. Seeing from Norm Van Brocklin what it takes to prepare for a game.

"He was a great guy, very bright guy, a tough guy, and he didn't take any crap from anyone. He was crusty outside, and he expected a lot out of everyone. He'd give everyone hell if they didn't give it to him. He was the coach of the Eagles. There were no coaches down there with Van Brocklin looking at film."

On one level, Madden was learning tidbits of the veteran's wisdom, for instance, "Let your backs and receivers do what they do best in taking advantage of the other defense"—an idea that would serve Madden well when he got to the Oakland Raiders.

On another level, Van Brocklin, who would lead his Eagles to the NFL title two years later, taught Madden how to see the big picture, literally. Until then, as an offensive lineman, Madden's vision of the field had been limited to watching only the defensive guy across from him.

"But now I'm seeing what's happening downfield, in the hole; I'm seeing the wide receivers, the running backs, flare control."

When the Eagles finally released him, he turned down an offer from the new Los Angeles Chargers of the fledgling American Football League because he knew he'd never be an effective player again; his leg would never fully heal, and he didn't want to take their money under false pretenses.

Besides, by now Madden knew he was going to be a coach. "By then I had a doctorate in football because of Van Brocklin. Looking back, I couldn't have asked for anything better than that.

"Maybe [without the injury] I could have played fifteen years. That's what I wanted to do: play fifteen more years. Then at some point you meet with reality, and you're not going to play.

"If you look at it one way, I lost a year. On the other hand, it was the most important year of my life. By then, I knew I wasn't going to be a lawyer. I was going to be a coach. I should have known that all along, but I didn't."

He definitely knew by then that he didn't want to wear a suit to work. He decided to go back to Cal Poly to get his master's in education to be certified in-state as a teacher. Teaching was a perfect job for a guy who loved to talk and to meet new people from different walks of life with different interests.

There was another reason to return to Cal Poly: his girlfriend, Virginia Fields, was there, also earning her master's in education. They'd marry in 1959. They have two sons and five grandkids now and have been married almost sixty years.

CHAPTER 4

WHEN MADDEN RETURNED TO school, he had a whole new attitude about schoolwork. He began to buckle down and really think about being a teacher.

"Before, I'd always gone to school to play. Now I wanted to learn."

He got his state teaching credential. He got his master's degree. But he wasn't meant for the life of an academic.

Coaching was the field that would allow Madden to use his teaching skills best.

He just didn't know how it would happen. Then, some would say, he got lucky.

★ ★ ★

Part of getting a master's in education is teaching in "the field," which is teacherspeak for being in an actual classroom to learn how to be a teacher.

Here's where being ready for his first stroke of luck came in: Madden's first practice-teaching gig was at San Luis Obispo High, where, it turned out, the football coach had just left. The new one couldn't come in until the next fall.

No one was around to teach spring football at a school that took its football very seriously. So Madden did it.

The high school's athletic director was so impressed with Madden's spring practices that he put in a good word to the head coach of Allan Hancock College in Santa Maria, California. Madden got a job at the junior college as an assistant coach. In his first year, the Bulldogs went 10–0. By the third year, Madden was head coach. He'd landed his first head coaching job at a collegiate level. He was on his way.

True, the league wasn't too high level, but you have to start somewhere. After all, Vince Lombardi, the most famous coach in the history of the NFL, started out as an assistant coach at St. Cecilia High School in Englewood, New Jersey. It took eight years for Lombardi to ascend to the college ranks and another seven to get to the pros...and then, of course, to becoming legendary enough for the NFL to name its championship trophy after him.

★ VINCE LOMBARDI ★

In the mid-1950s, football was a second-rate professional sport. Games drew only small crowds, and they were not shown on national television. National Football League starters earned less than ten thousand dollars a year, and every player worked at least one off-season job.

Then a man named Vince Lombardi changed things. From Brooklyn, New York, he was an Italian American and a devout Catholic. Football was his passion. His wife even said he thought about football on their honeymoon.

In college, Lombardi played football for Fordham University in the Bronx, New York. His coaching career began at St. Cecilia's, a Catholic school in New Jersey. The year after he took over the head coaching job at St. Cecilia's, his team was named the top prep team in the nation.

That success led to coaching jobs at Fordham and then at the US Military Academy at West Point. After five years at West Point, he took a dream job: assistant coach for the New York Giants, in charge of the offense. The team was terrible, but within three years, with Lombardi coaching the offense and future Dallas Cowboys legend Tom Landry coaching the defense, the Giants won the NFL Championship.

But it wasn't until two years later that the team and the NFL hit the big time. The 1958 NFL Championship Game between the New York Giants and the Baltimore Colts, played in freezing rain at Yankee Stadium, has come to be known as the Greatest Game Ever Played.

True, it was a sloppy and fumble-filled contest, but it was tremendously exciting. The Colts, from the working-class port town in Maryland, were fighting mighty New York, recent champions.

Because of the length of the game, NBC was able to broadcast it to the West Coast. The ratings were off the charts! Professional football had taken a step toward being a big-league sport.

And even though Lombardi's team lost, that game made him famous. In 1959, he got his first head coaching job—for the Packers in Green Bay, Wisconsin.

The Packers had a losing record the year before. They went 7–5 in 1959, Lombardi's first year. As they started winning more, the Packers became more popular. The following year, New City Stadium—now known as Lambeau Field—was sold out. It has been sold out ever since. Green Bay fans loved Lombardi. They called him "the Pope" because of the deep Catholic faith he always held. In 1961, the Pope got those fans an NFL title, beating the Giants, 37–0. The following year, the Packers beat the Giants for the title again, 16–7.

For the next five years, Green Bay succeeded because of Lombardi's tough attitude. He demanded "nothing but acceptance" from his players. One former player was said to have recalled that "he treated all of us the same: like dogs." Lombardi is known for legendarily saying, "Winning isn't everything; it's the only thing."

Lombardi's team went on to win the first two championship games between the NFL and the AFL—the first two Super Bowls. In 1970, soon after Vince Lombardi died of cancer, the NFL decided to name the Super Bowl trophy in his honor.

Today, only one pro football coach with sixty or more victories has a higher winning percentage than Lombardi's: John Madden.

★ ★ ★

When you're starting out as head coach, it's important to keep learning. Lombardi himself led one of the lectures Madden attended. Even though he was in the midst of winning three straight championships, Lombardi gave off-season lectures. Back then, head coaches didn't make a lot of money.

The name of the talk that day? "The Green Bay Sweep." It was a running play where star Packers running back Paul Hornung ("the Golden Boy" from Notre Dame) would run to the right side, with both guards pulling and brawny fullback Jim Taylor leading the way.

Going into the classroom, Madden wondered how long a talk about one play could last.

The answer: eight hours.

At one point, sitting in the back row as always, Madden noticed that, up in the front, one guy was asking a lot of questions. It was Sid Gillman, a legend in his own right. He had revolutionized the passing game in the late fifties, starting to use true wide receivers to catch passes downfield instead of having quarterbacks just throw the ball to their running backs.

"I said to myself, 'There's something wrong. I'm in back...and Sid Gillman is up front?'" Madden said.

Madden moved to the front.

He'd stay there.

★ ★ ★

It was another seminar that opened the next door, the one that would take Madden to the big time. And it was another case of making your luck by being in the right place at the right time and being ready for it.

This one was led by John McKay. McKay had helped turn USC's Trojans around, leading them to an 11–0 season in 1962 that ended with a national championship. One of the keys to USC's success was the subject of McKay's seminar: the I formation. Until the early sixties, teams liked to line up in a T: two running backs flanked behind the quarterback so that one back would block for the other.

McKay had instituted the formation that's in use to this day, with the running back behind the quarterback, with the option of going to either side without tipping off the defense.

At this talk, Madden was right up front, so he could hear distinctly when someone asked McKay how he'd come up with it. McKay said, "I didn't. Don Coryell did. He's here. Stand up, Don." It turned out that in the fifties, Coryell had used the I formation at a couple of small colleges before joining McKay's staff.

"After the talk, like at all coaching clinics, the coaches run up to ask questions," Madden said. Everyone else rushed to talk to McKay. But Madden was looking at Don Coryell. "I thought, 'This guy is here all by himself.' So I went over and sat with him and introduced myself. He told me about the I formation. After that, we became friends."

The chemistry that led to their good friendship was a little unusual. A smile in public wasn't Coryell's usual expression, unlike Madden's. And unlike Madden, Coryell didn't love talking to everyone he met.

But it was a perfect teacher-student relationship. Madden was always looking for new ways to do things, to think one step ahead of the guy on the other side of the field.

In this respect, Coryell was a visionary.

When Coryell took over as head coach at San Diego State College, a strong program in the NCAA's College Division, he realized that a powerful running game—as in the I formation—wasn't going to work for him. He needed big linemen for that, but he couldn't convince the large athletes in Southern California to come down the coast to play for the Aztecs when they could play for the more glamorous schools, USC and UCLA, in Los Angeles.

So instead Coryell started developing offensive strategies that "aired it out"—the new term for throwing the ball for distance, and often. He was a pioneer of the downfield passing game that today dominates the game.

Soon after Madden had introduced himself at McKay's talk, Coryell came down to Allan Hancock to recruit one of Madden's players. Coryell wisely recruited from junior colleges, where, if the players weren't as gifted, they were hungrier.

The evening of Coryell's visit, Madden invited Coryell over to his house, where Madden had a chance to get to know the human being beneath that all-business demeanor.

"Don didn't like to go out in public," Madden said. Coryell's idea of a good time was sitting around with friends and telling stories.

"So that's what we did. That's when I first met

Don Coryell. There was no one with a bigger heart. He was such a good guy. But he was so serious and tuned in to football that sometimes he'd forget to eat. I'll never forget one time in his office, he's drawing up some plays and opens his desk drawer and pulls out an apple. It's half eaten, and it's rotten.

"'We can do this,' he's saying, 'or we can do that....'

"'Don, that's a rotten apple you're eating.'"

Coryell looked at the apple, tossed it into a trash can, and bent back to his work.

By now, Coryell and his wife had become friends with John and Virginia Madden. It wasn't just a matter of having football strategy in common, as well as an intense desire to win. It was about being friends. So when Coryell called, there was no question about accepting the offer: defensive coordinator of the Aztecs.

Defensive coordinator? But wasn't offense his focus?

"Heck, when Coryell recruited me as defensive coordinator, I was just interested in coaching everything"—and competing at the highest level. During practices, Madden, coaching the defense, was so successful at stopping his boss's offense that, after a while, Coryell would have his unit compete against a second-level defense.

"He was competitive; I was competitive," Madden said. "So now we'd get one end of the field and he took the other end. But we still got along. He liked what I was doing. Because in games, I got the ball back for him."

How was San Diego State's defense built? Why was it so effective?

"We were tough and fast. Always playing fast is the thing. You can't play this game slow."

★ ★ ★

Coryell tutored Madden in more than strategy. He taught Madden some things about what it really means to be an effective and admired coach. His most important lesson to Madden was how to understand that his players were *people*.

At this point, Madden was an eager student who wanted to know everything he could about football strategy. But he was still young and saw everything through his own lens. He was driven by a love of the game, but the "ego" side of the game also still drove him. He wanted to rise to the top.

By his own admission today, he was still "a jerk."

Then came one of the most important days in Madden's life.

One of Madden's jobs for Coryell was getting good jobs for his players, back in the day when the NCAA allowed football players to have extra jobs to supplement their incomes—a good recruiting tool to supplement a scholarship. In 1965, the best off-season summer job was being offered by an alumnus who worked for Pepsi. He had a prime job open for an Aztecs player. A big booster.

Madden took pride in being an ace recruiter. He could recruit the best athletes when he had good jobs to offer them. Now he had a terrific way to lure a sought-after recruit to his program... until the day Coryell came into his office to say that the Pepsi job should go to Rod Dowhower, the Aztecs' starting quarterback the previous two seasons.

But Dowhower had been cut. Madden didn't get it.

"I said, 'Don, he can't play!' I couldn't understand

that at first. How can you give the best job to a guy who isn't playing? How could you give the best job you got to a guy who can't help you anymore?

"I said, 'Don, you can't do this!' I was a jerk. I probably just wanted to test him if he really meant it. I thought, 'He can't really mean this!'"

But Coryell said, "John, his wife is going to have a baby."

That changed things. Suddenly, Madden was seeing the big picture.

Not just seeing downfield, as Van Brocklin had taught him. Seeing the big picture, people-wise. He gave the job to Dowhower.

"That's when I learned the biggest lesson I ever learned from Don Coryell," Madden said. "Winning is not what it's all about. It's what you can do for the person, not always what the person can do for you. If you can do something for them, you do it. And that you can win and still be a good guy. You don't have to be a jerk.

"Don taught me how to get along with players, because every player is different. That was the difference between Don Coryell and I. But I changed.

I did learn. But that was a hell of a lesson. This wasn't a little thing. It was a tipping point. That's when I learned that if a player plays for you—or ever played for you—you just do what's right, [even if] it's not what's gonna help you.

"I was thinking about how I was a strong recruiter. I was thinking about being able to tell my guys, 'We'll get you good jobs.' But Don was thinking of doing right by a guy who just got cut, and was married, and who had kids and needed a job."

★ ★ ★

From the start at San Diego State College, there was another mentor in Madden's life: the head coach who'd been fired before Coryell had taken the Aztecs job. The college had kept Paul Governali on board because he was more than a football guy. He was a scholar with a PhD from Columbia University, a master teacher of athletes. He became the head of the athletic department. His office was one floor below Coryell and Madden's, on the first floor of the athletic offices. And it was an office where Madden, the guy who loved to learn from the experts, liked to hang out. There was no friction between Coryell and the man he'd replaced, so Madden was free to hang out in Paul's office.

"He was a great guy," Madden said. "And he was a great football mind. We just talked football."

And he could take some credit, along with Coryell, for Madden's quick rise to becoming one of the best defensive coordinators for one of the up-and-coming College Division programs.

CHAPTER 5

IN 1964, MADDEN'S FIRST YEAR, when San Diego State went 8–2, his defense gave up seventy-one points in the *entire ten-game season.* In 1965, his defense gave up eighty-seven points. In the final three games, they gave up none (while Coryell's offense scored 114)—with all three games on the road, no less.

Entering 1966, the Aztecs were now a College Division powerhouse. And they were 6–0 after the first six weeks, coming off a major defeat of rival Fresno State in front of a nice crowd of 15,000 at the Aztec Bowl.

One day in November, Madden was feverishly

preparing for an opponent from a different league (literally): powerful North Dakota State. The Aztecs had never met the reigning NCAA College Division champions. The Bisons had lost only one regular-season game in the previous two years. The year before, in the Pecan Bowl, they'd trounced Grambling College and won the NCAA championship.

The day before the game, Madden wanted to plot out some defensive schemes for the powerful Bisons offense, but he was finding it hard to concentrate in his office. On that day, as always, his office was crazy. It was the place where players hung out, using the phone, picking up their game tickets for Saturday.

So, to get some peace, Madden had gone out to sit on a bench and sketch some plays. When a guy sat down and asked what he was doing, Madden figured it was just a football guy who wanted to talk football. Not just any guy: the former coach and current general manager and part owner of the Oakland Raiders. Who didn't know Al Davis?

★ ★ ★

★ AL DAVIS ★

Like Lombardi, Al Davis was a child of the Brooklyn streets. Sports—well, competition of any kind—was Davis's thing, whether he was playing tough street football or trying out for, but not making, his high school (Erasmus Hall) or college (Syracuse University) varsity teams. He was too small.

But like his future Raiders coach, Davis quickly turned his competitive nature into a coaching career. He'd watch the Syracuse practices to jot down the plays. Days after graduating, he landed an assistant job at Adelphi, a small college on Long Island in New York.

When he was drafted into the army, Davis became head coach of an army team at Fort Belvoir, in Virginia. Davis wore an officer's cap even though he wasn't an officer. He drove a car on the Belvoir base, and no one knew how he'd received permission. His team went 8–2–1 against other US Army squads—and beat national champion Maryland in a scrimmage!

That caught the attention of Colts coach Weeb Ewbank, who gave him a scouting position. His first full-time football job was coaching for the Citadel in South Carolina, which is probably where he got the idea for the slogan he wrote on every Raiders weekly game plan: on Sunday, "We go to war."

He would win a whole lot of games. Counting that second unofficial Super Bowl in 1968, the Raiders appeared in five Super Bowls and won three.

In the football community, the flashy and aggressive Davis was known for more than his winning records and blustery personality. He was best known among players for treating people of all races fairly. When Davis coached the Raiders, he scouted small black colleges. No other NFL team could have found Maryland State College, now called University of Maryland Eastern Shore, on a map. That's where Davis discovered the great Art Shell.

Davis was the first to draft a black quarterback in the first round, and the Raiders were among the AFL leaders in number of black players on the roster—one of the reasons the early Raiders were popular. "You'd look at the stands," tight end Bob Moore said, "and I'll bet you it was fifty-fifty black and white families watching a black-and-white football team down there—a team that was fifty-fifty black and white."

In 1963, Davis refused to let the Raiders play an exhibition game in a segregated stadium in Mobile, Alabama. When locals discriminated against black players days before the 1965 All-Star Game in New Orleans, Davis yelled at commissioner Joe Foss and demanded that the game be moved. It was held in Houston instead.

Today, Al Davis is probably best known for his rebellious streak. After losing out on becoming commissioner of the merged leagues, he became the NFL's rebel. He sued the league so he could move the Raiders to Los Angeles in 1982.

He won. Then, thirteen years later, he moved the team back. He was forever bucking the league's authority.

But the league never had a more memorable—and successful—rebel. Without Davis pushing for the new league, it's a good bet the AFL would not have survived.

Madden figured Davis had dropped down to San Diego State to scout players and wanted to shoot the breeze. "I thought we were two guys talking football. I wasn't trying to get a job or impress him. There wasn't an iota of that in there."

Davis explained that he and Governali were friends and that they'd both grown up in New York. Davis didn't tell Madden that when Davis had asked Governali if there were any potential good coaches at San Diego State to add to the staff of his own head coach, John Rauch, Governali had recommended Madden.

"He started talking to me, asking me about what

I was doing," Madden said. "I was kind of showing him, 'We're doing this, doing that.' North Dakota uses split T, and they take pretty wide splits. So I used a form of a wide tackle six, and I was gonna hit the gaps, because their gaps were so big, and get penetration.

"And Al said, 'Why don't you jump into the gap? Stay where you are, then at the last second, jump and hit it that way.' So I did put a little of that in."

The final score of the game was 36–0, San Diego State. The Aztecs won their final four games by a combined score of 104–27 and won the College Division national championship.

As soon as the season ended, Davis called. He said he wanted to hire Madden as a linebackers coach.

Madden was shocked. "I thought, 'They don't even know me.'"

The new hiring didn't exactly shake the football world.

The *Oakland Tribune* announced that he'd been hired with a story under the headline RAIDERS ADD AIDE FOR RAUCH.

He was still so unknown that the paper didn't even use his name.

That would change very soon.

★ ★ ★

They didn't have a lot in common.

Al Davis was a wisecracking kid from the streets of Brooklyn, New York. He could rub people the wrong way. And he had a huge ego. He more or less wanted the whole world to think he was the best thing that had ever happened to the game of football.

Madden? An easygoing guy who just loved the fun of the game.

But where it counted, they had everything in common.

Neither ever coached a game he didn't think he could win. And both of them loved to play.

For Davis, it had been tough pickup games of street basketball, or football, in Brooklyn until he couldn't make the team at Syracuse, and like Madden with the Eagles, he stuck around the team to hone his coaching skills.

He coached a team in the army before joining the staffs of the Citadel and USC. Then Sid Gillman offered Davis a gig as the ends (that would be wide receivers today) coach of the new Los Angeles Chargers, where Davis eventually took a liking to a football-savvy rookie defensive back named Bobby Beathard.

"He was a brilliant guy," Beathard said. "He had a phenomenal mind and a great football mind period." The Chargers won the AFL West in their first two seasons.

Meantime, up the coast, the Raiders weren't having quite as much fun in their first two years in Candlestick Park, the eventual home of the 49ers. In their second season, the Raiders lost their first two games by a combined score of 0–99. They lost twice to the Chargers by scores of 44–0 and 41–10.

The Raiders' owner, Wayne Valley, demanded a stadium for his team in Oakland or he'd take the team elsewhere. So in 1962, the Raiders played in a stadium of their own: a jerry-rigged, 20,000-capacity place called Youell Field, named for . . . an undertaker. Players likened it to a high school field. The food in the press box? Pickles.

After the Raiders went 1–13—they'd already run through three head coaches—Valley and his co-owners knew exactly whom they wanted: that cocky ends coach down the coast, whose players had caught a zillion passes against the Raiders.

In his first season, using a long passing game and a hungry, aggressive defense, Davis led the Raiders to a 10–4 record—including two victories over the Chargers, who had now moved to San Diego. He was quickly recognized as a visionary strategist.

★ AFL ★

In the late 1950s, professional football had grown. A Texas oilman named Lamar Hunt decided that it was time for another pro football league in the United States. He found a partner in Bud Adams, another Texas oilman, and in 1959 the American Football League was born.

The AFL's strategy was to find fans who weren't being served in large areas of the country.

The AFL put teams in Los Angeles, New York, and Oakland, which would compete with existing NFL teams in their areas. But it also brought teams to areas that had none—Boston, Buffalo, Denver, Dallas, Houston. The plan worked, allowing the league to take hold in its first season, 1960.

At first nobody from the NFL took the AFL seriously. But when players drafted by both leagues began to sign with the AFL, and NBC was broadcasting the games, the league grew more successful.

In 1966, Raiders coach Al Davis took over as the AFL commissioner. He vowed to put the NFL out of business. That's when NFL officials quietly approached the AFL about a merger. It was agreed in 1966 that the two leagues would become one, beginning with the 1970 season.

The first two title games between the AFL and its rival league weren't called Super Bowls. The contest was billed as the AFL-NFL World Championship Game. Most people didn't think the AFL was a worthy competitor for the NFL, and most football fans didn't think the game between the two leagues' best teams was worth paying attention to.

In 1967, for the first World Championship game between Vince Lombardi's dominant Packers and the Kansas City Chiefs, the Los Angeles Memorial Coliseum was nearly half-empty. The NFL's Packers crushed the Chiefs, 35–10. Only a few reporters were there. The second game, between the Raiders and the Packers, filled Miami's Orange Bowl, and it was another victory for the NFL.

But then, with the merger two seasons away, the AFL proved once and for all that it was just as good as the NFL. A few days before the first official Super Bowl, New York Jets quarterback Joe Namath brashly "guaranteed" that his team would knock off the mighty Baltimore Colts— and it did. The following season, Hunt's Chiefs beat the NFL's Vikings.

In 1970, the leagues finally joined. The AFL became part of the NFL. The teams that had been in the AFL, along with three teams from the NFL, became a new NFL division, the American Football Conference (AFC). Now the champions from the AFC play the champions from the National Football Conference (NFC) in the Super Bowl each year.

★ ★ ★

In 1966, as the two leagues were getting ready to merge, Wayne Valley nominated Davis to become the commissioner of the AFL. Davis would settle for nothing less than making the AFL more powerful than the established NFL, or even put it out of business.

Davis was voted in. One of his first calls went to Madden's old roommate Bobby Beathard. "I'm going to put together some guys to scout the colleges," Davis, ever the competitor, told Beathard.

"We're going to find the best guys and hide them from the NFL."

But when the leagues did merge, NFL commissioner Pete Rozelle won the battle for the commissionership. Davis returned to Oakland to become part owner and general manager of the Raiders.

He'd chosen assistant coach John Rauch as the new head, and Rauch brought instant respectability. In 1967, he took the team to the second NFL-AFL title game (later known as Super Bowl II), although Lombardi's powerful Packers crushed them.

But while Rauch was having success on the field, he and Davis never got along. Davis—two years younger than Rauch—was too hands-on for Rauch, given to showing up at practice and telling receivers how to run their routes.

The 1968 season ended with a stunning loss to the underdog New York Jets in the playoffs. Rauch surprised Davis by immediately quitting and packing his bags for Buffalo. The Bills were a struggling team owned by the quiet, humble hometowner Ralph Wilson—the opposite of Al.

Davis told his coaching staff not to worry: "You'll

all have jobs," he said, "and if anyone wants to throw their hat in the ring for the head coaching job, let me know." Madden let Davis know right away.

At the ripe old age of thirty-two, he would be the youngest head coach in pro football, where the average age of a head coach was forty-two. A half dozen coaches were fifty or older.

"I went and told him, 'I know this team,'" he said. "I said to him, 'I know this team. I know these players. I know what they can do, and I know how to get them to do it.'

"I had a plan, because I had been thinking about this basically all my coaching life. Even as an assistant, I'd thought as a head coach. Not second-guessing, first-guessing."

And Davis wasn't worried that Madden was all of thirty-two?

"I said to him, 'Age is a number. If you're made to be a head coach, you'll be successful whether you're thirty-two, forty-two, or fifty-two. I don't have to wait ten years. I know I can be a head coach.'"

Today, Madden likes to joke about why Davis hired him. ("Maybe he ran out of guys.") But the real reason is that Madden had served as more than a linebackers coach. In 1969, teams didn't have dozens of coaches. They had only a handful, and each one had a lot of duties.

A linebackers coach on an NFL team today has one duty: prepare the players at his position. But when Madden held that title, he had much more influence on the team. The middle linebacker called the defensive plays, and so Madden was actually calling the defensive plays.

Just as important, there was no special-teams coach in those days. So that was part of Madden's job, too. Today, special teams are considered as important as offense and defense.

★ SPECIAL TEAMS ★

When the NFL first started, there were no "special teams." Today's football teams have different kickers for different kinds of kicks; back then a team's kicker was someone who played another position but also happened to be the best kicker. He would handle both kick-offs and field goals. Sometimes he was even the punter.

The player who snapped the ball back to the holder on extra points? He was the regular center, doing extra duty. Same with the kick returner: the fastest running back or wide receiver on the team would play that role.

Basically, there was nothing "special" about the kicking plays in the early days of professional football. They were the boring plays that happened when the teams changed possession of the ball.

In fact, the general managers and coaches in charge of putting their teams together didn't even think about getting players who might be all that good on the kicking plays, because no one thought those plays really mattered when it came to winning the game. Even though there were as many as thirty rounds in the draft back then (and just a dozen or so teams), no team would spend a draft pick on a player because he might be good on kicking plays.

But these days, even though there are only seven rounds in the draft (seven chances for a team to acquire a college player), every team drafts at least one or two players who probably won't be starters on offense or defense but are worth drafting because they'll stand out on special teams.

Special teams are as important now as the offenses and defenses, and good special teams are often the difference between winning and losing. Every season, many games are decided by last-second field goals. At the same time, there have never been as many punts returned for touchdowns as in the recent era. (Likely future Hall of Famer Devin Hester, who retired in 2016, was never much of a pass receiver, but he returned a remarkable fourteen punts for touchdowns in his career, as well as five kickoffs for touchdowns.)

Why are they called special teams? Because

today nearly every position on these teams is "specialized."

For instance, when one team tries an onside kick—a short kickoff that the team hopes to recover itself—the other team fields its "hands team," the players who are the best at catching and holding on to the ball.

And on extra points and field goal attempts, the defending team puts in a special group of players, including the linemen who are tall and have long arms, to try to block the kick.

A couple of special-teams players are so important that they can make great careers doing very specialized things. New York Giants' "long snapper" Zak DeOssie, who isn't a regular center, has played since 2007, mostly because he can "long snap" to kickers—and he has two Super Bowl rings to show for it.

And former Buffalo Bills wide receiver Steve Tasker put together a memorable career as the "gunner" on punting teams. The gunner's job is to "gun" down the field and tackle the punt returner—one of the hardest jobs in the game. ("You're trying to beat two guys in what amounts to a running street fight at a sprint," Tasker once said.)

Special teams are so important that talented special teamers who don't play on offense or defense can be just as proud of contributing to a win as anyone else on the team.

Basically, in his two years as linebackers coach, he was in charge of two-thirds of the team that Rauch had taken to two division titles.

So if you count the sit-down on that bench at San Diego State as the first interview, he nailed this one. Davis had his man.

This time, the *Oakland Tribune* gave him the top headline—although he was still second fiddle to one of his heroes: RAIDERS NAME NEW COACH; PACKERS LOSE LOMBARDI.

And they still didn't use his name in the headline! It was a few days later when the *Tribune* finally put his name above a story: MADDEN: A MYSTERY MAN.

He was no mystery to Al Davis.

"He knew both offensive and defensive football," Davis said. "He also had a feel for the passing game"—thanks, Don Coryell. "I also liked the idea that he was younger than me."

But Davis knew he was taking a big chance. Betting on a kid who fails opens you up to the old-school criticism that you should have hired a former head coach or at least a defensive coordinator.

"I thought he would be a great coach," Davis said, shrugging. "Anyone can see what a player is doing or not doing at the time; it was what you see in the future that matters: Can he coach? Can you develop him? It's about the relationship. It's about keeping me informed, and vice versa. It's like a marriage. Believing in one another."

His new hire was a quick learner, Davis said.

"At the beginning, my role was one of direction. Then it became one of assistance."

Before long, he recognized in Madden a couple

of things that they shared: a competitive urge that burned . . . but also a love of playing games that they'd kept at since childhood.

"We were like kids," Davis said. "We had our dreams. We were smart enough to know we wanted the same thing"—to win, and win by outthinking the other guy.

"When we met in our offices, it wasn't like I'm going into an inner sanctum to see the Man. It was just two guys talking. He was a friend.

"A lot of people think of Al Davis as the later Al Davis," Madden said. "They don't remember Al as what he was—just a guy. He was a young guy like me. He'd only head coached for three years.

"We used to have a box at the Coliseum during A's games in the off-season, and we'd work during the day, and at night the coaches would leave, and Al and I would go to the game, watch three or four innings, talk, and go have dinner."

If Davis chose the restaurant, they'd head to Francesco's, an old-world Oakland institution where Davis had his favorite table. Madden, a man of simple tastes, would have preferred a low-key Mexican place. He was a lover of basic cuisine, from burgers to ribs, but Mexican was, and still is, his favorite.

"We did a lot of talking at A's games. All football."

The new twosome brainstormed ways to get an advantage by thinking outside the box, one step ahead of everyone else. Among their innovations? The Raiders scouted low-profile colleges where no other team looked for recruits. They were the first team to film practice and the first team to have off-season rookie camps to help players learn how to play football the Raiders way.

★ ★ ★

But it wasn't only Madden's mastery of strategy that had won him the job. It was his ability to get to know the learning style of each and every player, the better to motivate him. Maybe it was because he'd studied to be a teacher.

Davis didn't want a drill sergeant. He once told Ron Wolf, who would later become the Raiders' key guy for scouting personnel, that he was not critical of his players, because he himself was never good enough to play the game. He had the utmost respect for his players, and he wanted a guy who could instill respect and loyalty by having that same respect. He knew that Madden was that guy.

For Madden, this was a new kind of mentor. Van Brocklin was a tutor in the strategy of the game and the importance of having a work ethic. Coryell taught him that football players were people, too.

Now he was working for a man whose love of competition and fierce desire to win matched his own.

"They had a culture about them," Madden's childhood friend John Robinson said, now from the perspective of a coach who had succeeded at every level. "Every team that really wins year in and year out and has a championship team builds a culture, has a culture. Sometimes winning destroys that, and everyone no longer adheres. But they did. They had a Raiders way.

"Al was responsible for it, and then John came

in and took it further, by establishing a camaraderie that was unique. The Raiders way wasn't about stats. It was about playing the game and winning the game. And it was about keeping the thing together."

CHAPTER 6

THESE DAYS, NOT A single member of the seventies Raiders wouldn't mention how much his relationship with his coach meant to his own motivation, and how much effort Madden put into making every player feel that he was important to the mix, from stars to reserves.

For a special teamer, it might be coming in early to the locker room and seeing Madden sitting on a stool reading the sports section and asking the player, "Hey, did you see this? Whaddaya think?"—and being surprised that the coach was asking his opinion about something: "He's treating me like a person, not a piece of meat?"

For the starting quarterback, it might be his coach saying, during a time-out in the key drive of the game, "Hey, call your play. You're the one out there—not me."

Defensive lineman Pat Toomay, one of Madden's favorites, was unusual. He was a brain. His dad worked on defense schemes—as a major general in the air force, as in Defense Department nuclear strategies. Pat majored in applied mathematics at Vanderbilt and, years later, would compare these Raiders to the ancient Greeks' heroes. They could be good and bad at the same time.

In other words, they were human. When Toomay decided to play the pro game instead of writing and philosophizing, he found himself in a Dallas Cowboys uniform being treated like meat.

Then, when he got to Oakland, it was the opposite. "I had a coach who put himself in my shoes, and in everyone's shoes. You never get that from other coaches."

"I used to talk to every player every day," Madden said. "It's not, 'I have to talk to Toomay.' It's, 'I have to talk to everyone.'" That was due in part to his being, then and now, an endlessly curious guy, always fascinated by other people's lives.

"Everyone is different," Madden said. "That was the thing that you learn. The way you teach, you have to adjust everything you do to the individuals. In teaching, you always have your ten. You have your bottom ten in everything. So this is just teaching—until your bottom ten get it, you don't have it.

"It doesn't mean they're not as smart. It's just that people all learn differently. Some learn by seeing pictures. Some learn by reading. Some learn by seeing it. Some learn by doing it, by walking through it. You have to do all those things and start everyone at the beginning."

★ ★ ★

For sure, you had to be a special kind of teacher to motivate one of the craziest, strangest, and most likable cast of football characters in history. There were a lot of different buttons to push.

Who was in this lovable band of brothers? Not your normal athletes. They were every kind of football personality you can think of. They were pretty far out on the fringe for the average NFL locker room.

Take Ted Hendricks, for instance. He was a true star at linebacker—long-armed, fast—but he was known almost as much for his antics. You never knew what practice was going to be like with Hendricks around. One day, in training camp, he arrived on the field on a horse, wearing a helmet and carrying a traffic cone as a lance.

Hendricks rode the horse to midfield and dismounted.

"That's nice, Ted," Madden said calmly. "Now, get rid of the horse."

On another occasion, Ted somehow found a large outdoor sidewalk umbrella and, with a white towel draped over his arm like a waiter, served refreshments after practice.

Then, there was linebacker Duane Benson, who got through tedious training-camp practices by playing trivia games with a teammate. His friend would spend the off-season compiling new brainteasers to stump him. Later, Benson would serve fourteen years in the Minnesota State Senate.

Not to mention the defensive back who played so intensely that after some games, he'd check himself into the hospital for two days of rest, even though he wasn't hurt...and would ride his motorcycle into the hospital.

Or the fullback who once rode his motorcycle from the back door to the front door of an Oakland bar.

But it should be noted that none of Madden's Raiders were ever in trouble with the law. For one thing, they respected their coach too much to mess up his reputation. Or embarrass him. When a coach trusts you as grown men to be professional and lets you do what you want during the week as long as you play your butt off on Sunday, you don't want to risk angering him. Madden had three simple rules: "Be on time, pay attention, and play like hell when I tell you to!"

The players' hijinks never crossed the line. In a very real way, they were like grown-up versions of Madden and Robinson's pals back in Daly City: all for one, one for all, and if you had to sneak into the drive-in or Seals Stadium, what was the harm if no one got hurt?

★ ★ ★

During the season, Madden's Raiders were less rascal-ish than during the summer training camp. Other teams trained at colleges, and the players slept in dorms. But Davis housed his team in the discount El Rancho Tropicana Motel up in the cowboy town of Santa Rosa, California—the middle of nowhere.

"Of course we stayed at the El Rancho," defensive lineman Dave Rowe said. "Nobody stays at something like that. Football teams stay in dormitories. We stayed at the El Rancho"—where curfews were routinely broken.

In fact, while most players dreaded midsummer training camp, some of the Raiders, like Ken Stabler and Fred Biletnikoff, told their wives that camp began earlier than it actually did—so they could meet up with their friends again.

One night, Madden was doing bed check. That evening, Biletnikoff, the Hall of Fame wide receiver, had decided to hit a few bars, so he put two tennis shoes under the covers, rolled up towels to look like legs, and took a table lamp and stuck it on the pillow, with his baseball hat instead of the shade.

At practice the next day, with the team gathered, Madden said, "By the way, Biletnikoff. I came in last night and your head lit up. Gonna cost you."

"I thought that was all normal, that other teams did that stuff, it was normal to me," Madden said. "I would have done the same thing, the things they did." He knew when to stop being serious and reveal his true, goofy sense of humor. Like the practice when a fight broke out on the goal line. He ran into the scrum flailing his arms, yelling, "That's not a fight! I'll show you to fight!"—like a cartoon character. Everyone broke up.

All in all, the mood was pretty light, and Madden could be as loose as his players. It was a common occurrence to see the head coach challenge his strength coach to races down the El Rancho's narrow driveway. Using the deceptive speed that always got him the lead, and the width of his butt to keep the other coach from passing him, Madden was unbeaten.

"Sometimes I think this is forgotten, but it's a

game," Madden said. "And if it's a game, I think it should be fun. That stuff I did with the Raiders and coaching was to have fun.

"I mean, in training camp, we asked them for a lot. We had a two-month camp. They were there so long. You knew you couldn't press too hard on the buttons. It was awfully fragile. I knew if I pressed too hard on the buttons, we'd have nothing. We'd have bleep."

The El Rancho summer camp had been such a legend that when the motel was about to be torn down decades later, a TV crew asked Madden to come up and narrate a short film about how the old days were disappearing.

Up behind the field he spotted a seven-man blocking sled. In the past, everyone had one, for offensive lines to learn how to jump out and block opponents as a team. By then, sleds had become old-school. But for Madden, they were a symbol of the great days.

"I couldn't go to sleep that night," he said. "I can't leave that seven-man sled up against a fence where they're going to build a Walmart. I got someone to get it and bring it to me. I have a seven-man sled in my parking lot."

Madden paused, then said, "I was a big seven-man sled guy."

★ ★ ★

As punter Ray Guy put it, "John has a great mind, but very few great minds make great coaches. John's strength was that he had a way of making it simple. Whatever he was teaching us wasn't complex, something you couldn't understand.

"They're individuals during the week. What it boils down to is, on Sunday, they eventually become a team."

The loose, innocent-outlaw vibe of the team was a perfect fit for a working-class city that was the largest West Coast port in the country. Raiders fans were wild and passionate. And some were pretty famous. Sonny Barger, the head of an infamous motorcycle club in Oakland, and Bobby Seale, the leader of the notorious Black Panthers, would show up at practice at the invitation of players.

"They were just testing me," Madden said.

But he was more than happy to welcome another "outlaw"—famed country singer Willie Nelson, who would come to Raiders games when he was touring through Northern California.

(Nelson the prankster would get the best of Madden a few years later, when he invited John and Virginia to a concert, with seats on the stage . . . and then surprised Madden by making him sing "Amazing Grace," even though Madden didn't know some of the words. A year later, Nelson asked him to another concert, and this time Madden was ready . . . except Nelson told the crowd, "He's going to sing 'The Yellow Rose of Texas.'")

Defensive back George Atkinson, a Raiders legend, might have summed it up best: "You had to take your hat off to Madden as far as keeping everything from going haywire bonkers, you know?"

★ ★ ★

His guys may have had a little more wildness to them than the average team, but Madden, unlike most coaches, didn't try to stamp it out. Other teams tried to come off as formal and organized, like Hank Stram's Kansas City Chiefs, who had to wear bright red blazers when they traveled.

The Raiders were just a band of down-to-earth brothers who took pride in being part of a universal friendship. They wore jeans when they walked through airports.

"Those guys drove pickups," Robinson said. "They drank beer, ate hamburgers, and dressed in jeans. They weren't slick. They hung out together a lot. They were guys who were like John and I. They had just loved sports, and that's all they did. They were just *guys*."

The nicknames they affectionately gave each other said all you needed to know about the bond: King Arthur. Foo. Snake. Rooster. Boomer. Piggy. The Governor. The Hit Man. Fog. Scrap Iron. Assassin. Tooz. Stump. Dr. Death. Ghost. Kick 'Em. Buckethead.

"He had an uncanny ability to deal with these eccentric guys," Robinson said. "We talked about it all the time. He brought a camaraderie that was really unique."

The Raiders were all just a bunch of guys. They hung out. There was a camaraderie because they knew that the game matters more than anything. They knew about camaraderie.

★ ★ ★

Madden had been given his own nickname, of course.

On the sidelines, in the short-sleeved shirt that was always coming untucked over his somewhat stout belly, tie askew, blond hair flapping, his arms flailing, Madden seemed to be screaming at the refs on every other play, his pale redhead's face turning bright red.

So not for nothing had his team given him the affectionate nickname Pinky.

He didn't like it much. But somewhere inside he smiled, knowing it was a term of endearment.

CHAPTER 7

FOOTBALL HISTORIANS USUALLY SAY that Madden's Raiders had the best win-loss record of the 1970s because they had great players who had a good coach. They had Hall of Famers. How could you lose?

But something that didn't make it into the record books accounted for some of the motivation that would lead them to the top of the league: being on the wrong end of a controversial decision in what NFL Films calls "the most famous play in modern NFL history."

In legend, it's called the Immaculate Reception. To the Raiders, it was the Immaculate *De*-ception. And it was famous for all the wrong reasons.

★ ★ ★

Madden's first three years had been tantalizing. The Raiders were powerful, but they couldn't win the Lombardi Trophy.

In the first year, 1969, the team went 12–1–1 and knocked off the Houston Oilers, 56–7, in the first round of the playoffs. But then the Raiders lost to their archrival, the Kansas City Chiefs, whom they'd beaten twice during the regular season. The Chiefs went on to win the Super Bowl.

Madden was named the Pro Football Writers' AFL Coach of the Year. The award didn't mean a lot in light of losing to the Chiefs.

In 1970, the Raiders went 8–4–2, sneaking into the playoffs before losing to the Baltimore Colts in the championship game. The next year was another 8–4–2 season, but no playoff appearance. But Davis's draft that year laid a foundation for future success. First pick Jack Tatum would become all-world. Chosen in the second round, Phil Villapiano grew into one of the most overachieving and beloved players in Raiders history. And running back Clarence

Davis, the fourth-round pick, would be pivotal in the success of years to come.

The spark had been lit. The next year, the fan was flamed by a single play.

★ ★ ★

It was December 23, 1972: a day that no Raiders fan, or coach, will ever forget. Madden hasn't. It still angers him.

In 1972, they'd dominated the AFC West with a 10–3–1 record. Their first playoff opponent was the Steelers, who hadn't made the playoffs in modern times—until third-year quarterback Terry Bradshaw began to blossom and led Pittsburgh to an 11–3 record.

It figured to be close—and it was. Both defenses were on their game. The Steelers led, 6–0, on two field goals, before Madden decided to throw backup quarterback Kenny Stabler into the game. Stabler pulled off an unlikely thirty-yard touchdown run that seemed to seal the deal, 7–6, with 1:13 left.

That's when it got crazy. Two Bradshaw completions got the ball to the Steelers 40. On fourth and 10, with 22 seconds left, Bradshaw scrambled and threw a pass to Frenchy Fuqua.

The ball was arriving in Fuqua's arms just as Raider Jack Tatum slammed him from behind. The ball popped out, going backward. Steelers halfback Franco Harris plucked it out of the air a few inches above the ground and ran to the end zone.

In 1972, a pass wasn't legal if it hit the hands of two offensive players, but if it bounced off a defender, it was a good catch. The referee, Fred Swearingen, didn't signal a touchdown. As fans mobbed the field, Swearingen called his crew together, and Madden ran onto the field.

"Just get off the field," Swearingen said. "We don't know what happened."

"I *know* you don't know what happened!" answered Madden.

For most of the national television audience, it was the first time they were exposed to Madden's sideline temper. Not surprisingly for a guy who didn't even allow himself to consider that he might ever lose a game, Madden didn't have much control of his emotions when he thought the refs had made a bad call. With his arms flailing like some crazy octopus, his hot-tempered sideline tantrums soon became a thing of legend.

★ ★ ★

Swearingen called upstairs to Art McNally, the ref's boss, then came out and signaled "Touchdown!" According to Swearingen, the ball had hit Tatum, and not Fuqua. It was a legal reception.

But it wasn't. It shouldn't have been a legal play.

There are two sources for this conclusion. One is former *San Francisco Examiner* writer Frank Cooney, who taped the telecast and saw during the closing scroll of credits a shot from the end zone: "It was really clear," he said. "Fuqua reached out for the ball, and it hit him in the arm as Tatum hit him from behind."

The other? Fuqua himself, according to Raiders tight end Raymond Chester, who'd been a teammate of Fuqua's at Morgan State.

"Frenchy came into our locker room after the game," Chester said a few years ago, "and leaned over my locker and said, 'It hit me.' 'It hit me'—he absolutely told me that in the locker room."

No team likes to lose on what they think—and actually was—a blown call.

Now take a team driven by an owner and a coach who cannot stand to lose.

The motivation was in place. The players were primed. And the coach was coming into his prime.

★ ★ ★

In 1973, the Raiders went 9–4–1 behind a running game that had no equal in the league. Madden's love of building a team around his blockers paid off big-time. Madden's running backs gained 2,510 yards rushing that year.

In the modern pass-oriented game, a team gaining more than a hundred yards rushing in a game is a good day on the ground. That year, running mostly behind Gene Upshaw and Art Shell (the future head of the NFL Players Association and a Raiders head coach, respectively), the backs averaged 179 yards running per game.

No matter how good his skill players were,

Madden would always love the linemen who did the blocking.

"Guys who get chosen as head coaches now are in the finesse art of the game: strategists, and not the guys who coach the offensive line," Robinson said. "I always say, 'Be careful of the finesse part of the game. It's the physical part that determines who wins.'

"John loved the lines. Those were his guys. He was very smart about the physical part of the game. He knew that the game was won or lost in that area. That's where you had to find guys—for the lines.

"But back then, the draft wasn't very scientific, so if your uncle lived in Youngstown, Ohio, you might grab a lineman from Youngstown State. But since John knew how to teach, since he was a really good teacher, he could teach an offensive line. That's why his lines flourished."

Playing physically became Madden's Raiders' stock in trade. Upshaw would wrap his forearm in tape and padding so that when he blocked, he was using, basically, a cast. For Villapiano, the line-backer, no play was a real play unless someone shed blood: his opponent or him. The defensive backs figured you had to hit a receiver hard enough that even if he caught the ball, he wouldn't want to catch it anymore.

"When you played the Raiders," Robinson said, "they were going to kick your butt."

★ ★ ★

The 1973 game that still stands out in the Raiders' minds was the December 8 game against the Chiefs in the Coliseum. Hank Stram's Chiefs had ridden an absolutely huge defensive line to a 6–4–2 record. If they could knock out the 7–4–1 Raiders at home, they'd have a half-game lead going into the final two weeks for the division lead.

It wasn't even close. The Raiders' running backs ran roughshod over the Chiefs, whose own best running back was held to a single yard. The Raiders won, 37–7.

That's not what those Raiders remember, though. They remember the best Chiefs-Raiders free-for-all of all time. In those days, the game didn't have as many rules about fighting. Emotions boiling over when the Raiders met the Chiefs were expected.

This rumble was one for the books. Chiefs running back Ed Podolak had been running out of bounds when Atkinson hit him a little late. Well, a lot late. Meantime, Villapiano laid a hard hit on running back Jeff Kinney and had to roll under a bench to keep from getting kicked by a bunch of Chiefs.

At that point, a friend of Villapiano's, a mail carrier from back home in New Jersey, dove over a snow fence to join in before the security guys threw him into the mud. Then a Chiefs defensive back broke up the scrum by dumping Gatorade on everyone. It worked out the way it always did back then: no penalties, no harm, no foul.

The Raiders' momentum lasted into the first round of the playoffs, where the Raiders wreaked revenge on the Steelers, 33–14. As usual, a dominant running game prevailed (Kenny Stabler threw just seventeen passes, completing fourteen). The turning point was an interception return for a touchdown by Willie Brown.

Next up? The Super Bowl–defending Dolphins. In an added twist to the drama for this game, the Dolphins' director of pro personnel was none other than Madden's old college roommate, Bobby Beathard. Bobby was now in his second year in charge of building a team for Hall of Fame coach Don Shula.

With the Baltimore Colts in the sixties, Shula had become known as one of the league's top coaches. He'd lost to Joe Namath's Jets in Super Bowl III—two weeks after those Jets had beaten the Raiders in John Rauch's last Raiders game. But Shula had rebounded to turn the Dolphins into an elite team: tough and bruising.

Beathard denied having any advice for Shula as he prepared to take on Beathard's old buddy. But whatever the reason, the Dolphins, led by a bull of a running back named Larry Csonka, beat the Raiders, 27–10.

The three most important plays involved a tactic that no one had expected. Each time the Dolphins faced third and long, Shula circled both backs out of the backfield, luring the Raiders' linebackers with them . . . only to see quarterback Bob Griese, not the fastest guy in the world, run straight up the gut for first downs.

Madden had been outcoached, but there was no shame there. Don Shula would win his second consecutive Super Bowl that year and be elected to the Hall of Fame in his first year of eligibility.

By 1974, Madden's offensive line had solidified into the best in the league. Now it was time to build a defense. Madden had gotten his offensive lineman. Davis, though, had always believed that the defensive backfield was a team's most important unit.

Three-quarters of the gang were in place: captain Willie Brown, a cornerback, and safeties Tatum and Atkinson, two of the league's most savage tacklers. Now Skip Thomas, a seventh-round draft pick in 1972, emerged as the fourth starter—and the Soul Patrol was born. Thomas's nickname was Dr. Death because he practiced and played so hard that at the end of the day he looked as if he were ready to die.

"Skip was from his own world," Atkinson said.

"A unique individual," was Mark van Eeghen's opinion. Villapiano's take: "I wouldn't mess with Skip Thomas in a million years."

The Soul Patrol had their own poster, depicting the four of them in menacing poses, and their own territory: they'd mark off a section of the locker room with tape that no one was allowed to cross. By the end of the season, both Atkinson and Tatum had four interceptions. Dr. Death had six.

That season, Madden's Raiders went 12–2, thanks in part to the emergence of a speedy receiver named Cliff Branch. Teams couldn't double-team Biletnikoff anymore. Branch had such speed that team personnel honcho Ron Wolf said, "When Cliff got even, he was leavin'."

The 1974 playoffs brought a chance for sweet revenge against the Dolphins. It all came down to a single play forever known afterward as the Sea of Hands.

With thirty-five seconds left and Miami leading 26–21, the Raiders were on the Dolphins 8. First down. Stabler faded. Every receiver was covered. Clarence Davis, the running back with notoriously bad hands, was supposed to just circle around to the left. But the Dolphins defensive end was sacking Stabler from behind. As he was going down, Stabler caught a glimpse of black amid all the white, in a sea of hands: Davis surrounded by two Miami defenders.

The Dolphins' Mike Kolen got a hand on the ball, and it popped into the air. Davis grabbed at it and juggled it—just as defensive back Charlie Babb slammed into him—squeezing the ball between the two of them.

Davis came away with it for the touchdown. "It was the most significant win for the franchise ever," tight end Bob Moore said.

In the Dolphins locker room, Shula cried.

But perhaps the Raiders had left too much emotion on the field. The next week, the Steelers ran all over them and easily won, 24-13.

★ ★ ★

"The better you get," Madden said, "the more you expect to win. And I don't ever remember coaching a game I thought I was going to lose. I swear to god.

"With the highs of winning, you're not equipped to lose. That low is tremendous.

"The expectation is up there, and when you miss, man, that's a shot in the gut."

★ ★ ★

In 1975, a new coach was on the Raiders roster. Madden knew him pretty well.

Childhood friend John Robinson and John Madden had always had a pact: whoever becomes a head coach first hires the other guy. But when Davis hired Madden in 1969, Robinson was doing well at Oregon and stayed on the college path. He was at USC under John McKay when he decided it was time for a change.

Madden eagerly hired him as his running backs coach. The Daly City kids were back together.

Robinson quickly noticed something different about his friend as they drove to work each day: he was no longer curious about everything that was happening in the world. He'd changed. He was totally focused on his job.

"It was true," Madden said. "John would ask me, 'What do you think about this or that,' and I didn't even know about it."

But Madden's intense focus still hadn't taken his squad to the finish line.

For the first *Monday Night Football* game of the 1975 season, the Raiders played the Dolphins in Miami. The Raiders won and put together a seven-game winning streak on the way to a division title.

The first round of the playoffs led to a match against the upstart Cincinnati Bengals, who had finished 11–3. If the Raiders won, they'd get another shot at the Steelers. Behind four sacks from linebacker Ted Hendricks, they won.

But for the Raiders, the game against the Steelers saw them playing with kind of a stacked deck. A week of rain and snow and freezing rain had left the field at Three Rivers Stadium a mess. The night before the game, for reasons still debated by conspiracy theorists, the tarp blew off, and a heavy wind froze the whole field.

When the game started, the only part of the field you could play on was the middle. The ten yards on each sideline were unplayable. That took away the passing game. The Steelers won a hard-fought, fumble-filled, but unforgettable game, 16–10.

Afterward, Madden made no excuses. "That's just part of football," he said.

Robinson's instinct to get out of town paid off. In 1976, he got the USC head coaching job . . . and went to four Rose Bowls, and won a national championship, before taking over the lowly Los Angeles Rams and taking them to two conference championships.

★ ★ ★

The schedule-makers knew a good matchup when they saw it. In 1976, the Steelers were the Raiders' first opponents. And the Raiders were ready to make a statement.

"The two Super Bowls they went to were through us," Villapiano said. "We couldn't take it anymore. Here come the Steelers all cocky. We were going to leave it out there. If we don't win that day, forget the season. We put it all out on the line."

The Steelers led, 21–7, halfway through the fourth

quarter, but the Raiders felt as if Pittsburgh might be taking the outcome for granted. "In our huddle," tackle John Vella said, "we just said, 'Keep doing it. Keep doing it.'"

Stabler found Biletnikoff for a touchdown. A recovered fumble led to another TD. A blocked punt led to still another. An interception led to the winning field goal. The Steelers had been vanquished. It was a promising start.

After winning two more games, the Raiders lost to the New England Patriots, 48–17, in the fourth week. It was a wake-up call.

They didn't lose again.

The Raiders finished the regular season 13–1 before facing the Patriots in the first round of the playoffs. After three quarters, they were losing, 21–10. They rallied to win, 24–21, and advanced to the conference championship, where they would face...the Steelers.

The third time proved the charm because of Madden's beloved offensive line, the Soul Patrol, and three running backs grinding out an impressive total of 166 yards. The success of the running game allowed the offense to control the clock. The rested defense held the Steelers to seventy-two yards rushing and forced Bradshaw into a pitiful 44.5 quarterback rating on fourteen of thirty-five passes.

"We were ready, man," said Villapiano. "We absolutely nullified everything they did. And we were in the Super Bowl!"

CHAPTER 8

AFTER ITS HUMBLE BEGINNING in the first few years, the championship game between the National Football Conference and the American Football Conference had become not only must-watch television, but nearly a national holiday. And Madden's Raiders were front and center, ready to play for the Lombardi Trophy in one of the most storied football stadia in the land: the hallowed Rose Bowl, in beautiful Pasadena, California.

The week before the game, the cover of *Time* magazine, which was the nation's weekly cultural bible back then, devoted its cover to THE GREAT AMERICAN SPECTACLE.

Today, even the most fanatic fan would be hard-pressed to name the winner of, say, Super Bowl XV, but in 1976, only ten games had been played, and three teams—Green Bay, Miami, and Pittsburgh—had won six of them.

The club of Super Bowl winners was a very special club. The winner of the eleventh would make real history in the annals of the game—and its players would forever have a place in history.

Today, the game's a year-round business, and the athletes and coaches who win the big game hardly get time to savor their amazing accomplishment. The players have to take part in off-season camps. The coaches have to immediately start to prepare for the following season, knowing that the league is going to give them a tough schedule that will begin with the season's first high-profile game against a tough opponent.

But when more than a hundred thousand people filed into the Rose Bowl that sunny day, the stakes were huge. The winner would reach the pinnacle of American success stories. The loser would be forgotten.

In 1976, there weren't off-season camps, or

organized team activities, or minicamps, or rookie camps, so the off-season was long. Super Bowl winners could relish their triumph. They could relax, knowing they were the best in the world, and hang in their hometowns as local heroes.

Winning the Super Bowl today is great. Winning it a decade after the game began was huge.

Madden, a man who never coached a game he thought he would lose, had always expected he'd make it to the big one. When he did, he made sure he'd be prepared.

He knew how to make his luck.

★ ★ ★

The Minnesota Vikings were led by popular, handsome, camera-ready quarterback Fran Tarkenton. He didn't have a big arm, but he'd made up for it by becoming the first scrambling quarterback. He'd taken the Vikings to the Super Bowl on a short passing game (averaging just seven yards per pass) and handing the ball off, or dumping it off, to his star running back, Chuck Foreman.

But he did have a big mouth. "We are going to go [to Los Angeles]," he told *Time* magazine, "[and] we are going to win."

None of the Raiders made predictions. They spent the next two weeks getting ready for the game of their lives.

Madden had been preparing since 1970, his first year as the head coach of the AFC Pro Bowl team. By the time his Raiders were poised to play in a Super Bowl, he'd coached four AFC all-star teams. And every year when he was coaching the all-stars, he'd go out of his way to ask any all-star who'd been in a Super Bowl: "What makes one team better than the other, psychologically?"

When you get to the Super Bowl, Madden had thought, both teams are pretty evenly matched. So, he reasoned, the team that had the mental advantage attitude-wise was better prepared.

For the week preceding the all-star game for those four years, he asked Super Bowl vets about how to prepare for the game. They told him that the more they could concentrate on football, and the less they were distracted by the craziness of the carnival atmosphere, the better they could prepare for the game.

In other words, if there were problems with hotel rooms, the practice field, media access, and tickets for friends, the players' minds weren't on the game. The two-week gap between the conference championships and the big game meant plenty of time for distraction.

So when he made it to the Super Bowl, Madden—in typical Madden fashion—was thinking differently than most coaches.

Until that year, head coaches usually used that first week to put the game plan in place. Then they'd let the players relax in the second week, when the coaches had to deal with the details.

Madden turned that plan on its head.

"So," he said, "the first week, I said, 'We're going to get everything out of the way.'"

He gave his players all their tickets and demanded they give them out that first week. He made sure every player had an extra seat on the plane and didn't limit the player's companion to a spouse. Girlfriends and moms were okay, too. He even got an extra hotel room for everyone: players and staff. Practices were light. Mostly, they watched film.

And the film suggested that the Raiders were well suited to face the Vikings. Minnesota's defense was anchored by a front four known as the Purple People Eaters (their colors were purple and gold), named after a gimmicky pop song from 1958.

They were fast and agile, but they were light. The defensive linemen Jim Marshall and Alan Page (a future Hall of Famer) weighed 248 and 245, respectively—about as much as a linebacker in the modern NFL.

Madden's offensive line, the best-coached unit on a team coached by an offensive lineman, out-weighed them. It looked as if the Raiders would be able to run.

On defense, Madden was using a three-four alignment, and the four linebackers would probably be able to handle Tarkenton's short passes—if, in fact, the Vikings didn't radically change their game plan.

But the Vikings coach was the stone-faced Bud Grant, who liked to play conservatively. As the *Los Angeles Times* writer Jim Murray put it, "The

Vikings play football like a guy laying carpet. The Raiders play like a guy jumping through a skylight with a machine gun."

The Vikings had made it this far by playing efficiently and relying on a special-teams unit that was the most opportunistic in the league. In the championship game against the Rams two weeks earlier, they'd blocked a punt and a field goal.

Still, Madden knew that even though his team looked good on paper, he had to make sure that his guys' heads were in a confident place. So he pulled another psychological trick: "Don't fear all the hype," he said. "Embrace it."

"He told us to treat it like a normal business trip," Stabler said, "and that we were going down to Los Angeles to take care of business."

Asked, "You didn't say, 'Men, you're about to play the biggest game of your life?'" Madden answered, "Shoot. That's the last thing I'd say."

The second week, Madden put the game plan into place: they practiced which plays they'd use against which Vikings defense, which defenses they'd use when the Vikings offense lined up a certain way.

The practices went very well. The practice Thursday, three days before the game, is remembered by Madden and the players as the best one the team had ever had. "That practice," Atkinson said, "was, man, like no other. We were crisp. Sharp. No mistakes." As Madden recalls it, not a single Stabler pass hit the ground.

On Saturday, Madden called the practice off after twenty minutes.

"Let's stop right now" is what fullback Pete Banaszak remembers his coach telling the team. "Go on in. If we play like this, we're going to kill them."

"I just knew that I liked the matchup," Madden said. "I liked the way we were prepared. I liked the game plan. I felt as confident as I've ever felt."

★ ★ ★

The Rose Bowl was filled to capacity: 104,594. The temperature was a balmy sixty degrees. Most fans were rooting for the Raiders.

Early on, it was close. The Vikings blocked a punt by Raiders Hall of Fame punter Ray Guy deep in the Raiders end. They were about to score the first touchdown when Villapiano forced a fumble at the goal line. With the Raiders' backs to the end zone on third and seven, the Vikings expected a pass. Madden called a run, mostly to give Guy some room for another punt. But Clarence Davis broke through the line and took the ball thirty-five yards. The Raiders drove down the field but had to settle for a field goal.

Madden was angry. But Stabler put his hand on his coach's shoulder and said, "John, don't worry. There's plenty more where that came from."

There was. And on the defensive side, the Vikings were powerless. It was 19–0, Oakland, in the third quarter. The Vikings never got closer than twelve points, and the final score, in a rout, was 32–14.

When the final second had ticked off, linebacker Ted Hendricks and lineman Charles Philyaw picked Madden up to put him on their shoulders. They carried him a few yards until—in typical Raiders fashion—they tripped over a photographer, and Madden tumbled to the ground.

In the locker room, "John's face was lit up like a Christmas tree," Banaszak remembered. "He was hugging everyone."

They'd won sixteen of seventeen games.

Now he'd done it all. What was next?

CHAPTER 9

TODAY, AFTER MORE THAN fifty Super Bowls, a coach winning just one isn't all that special. Lots of coaches have won one. To be judged as one of the greats these days, you have to win two or three or four.

But in 1976, winning one was as historic as it got. "Today, it's, 'How many rings can you get?'" Madden said. "But back then, that wasn't a thing."

And so over the next year, his ninth, Madden began to think of his endgame. There were lots of reasons. "I'd coached in every game, and I won every game there was, from rookie-camp games to preseason to regular season to playoff to championship to Super Bowl to Pro Bowl," he said. "And I thought, 'Shoot, all I can do is do it all again.' I thought, 'There's not one thing out there keeping me out there.'"

But what about walking away from all that money? Because in 1976, there wasn't any money. Coaches didn't sign multiyear, multimillion-dollar contracts.

"Also," Madden said, "back then you didn't look at it as your lifetime work. You looked at it as part of your life of coaching. If you got ten years on one team, it was a lot. That was a long time. Today, I would have been coaching a long time. Everyone else is. Then, no one was."

He wasn't going to walk away right after winning the big one, though. He had his eye on ten years. That was how long his idol, Lombardi, had coached, so he wasn't going to pull up short of the finish line.

★ ★ ★

In the meantime, the 1977 Raiders picked up where they'd left off: as a dominant team. They won eight of their first nine, including a defeat of the Steelers in Pittsburgh. They finished 11–3 before winning a thrilling overtime game over Baltimore in the first round of the playoffs.

But the Denver Broncos stopped them in the championship game, in part because of another controversial play that ranks a close second to the Immaculate Deception: the fumble that, all of a sudden, wasn't a fumble.

Denver was leading, 7–3, and was poised to score another touchdown, when Bronco running back Rob Lytle fumbled on the two-yard line. Raiders tackle Mike McCoy picked the ball up and, hearing no whistle, ran downfield, untouched...until he looked over and saw Madden slapping his forehead.

The refs called the play back and said there hadn't been a fumble. This was before the days of instant replay. Television tapes would later reveal that Lytle had clearly coughed the ball up, but the refs hadn't seen it until he hit the ground. Denver went on to win, and dreams of a second consecutive Super Bowl were dashed.

Madden entered the 1978 season, his tenth, knowing it might be his last. And then, in the preseason, something happened that changed his view of the game forever.

It was a meaningless exhibition game in Oakland against the Patriots. New England was finishing up a two-game exhibition trip on the West Coast. They'd played the Rams in Los Angeles the week before.

On one play, Patriots quarterback Steve Grogan overthrew receiver Darryl Stingley on a crossing route. Jack Tatum was heading for Stingley. When he saw that the pass had sailed high, Tatum turned his head to the left and led with his right shoulder pad, readying to collide with Stingley's chest.

But Stingley ducked, and his head slammed into Tatum's right shoulder pad. Stingley collapsed to the ground. His neck was broken.

He was strapped into a gurney and left the field.

For the rest of the game, Madden's thoughts were in two places: with the game, and with the player who'd been paralyzed.

And so, after the game, Madden visited the hospital, where he found out that the Patriots' doctor was nowhere to be seen; he'd flown back to Boston after the previous week's game.

Madden was told that only family members were allowed to visit. He found a way to get into a doctor's gown and snuck himself into Stingley's room, where he leaned down to assure Stingley that everything was going to be all right.

"And then," Pat Toomay said, "he saw that the intubator had slipped out of Stingley's nose. He ran to get someone to fix it. He saved Darryl Stingley's life."

Madden then called the airport and insisted that the Patriots' plane return so that someone from the team could get to Stingley's side.

"On that day, he revealed who he was," Toomay said. "A man with a heart."

★ ★ ★

If there had been any chance of Madden's prolonging his career, it ended with the worst record of his decade: 9–7, and no playoff appearance for the first time since 1971. A few days after the season, Madden told Davis he was retiring. He still had "gas in the tank . . . but there was nothing there anymore," he said. "I was done."

The gang would soon break up. Stabler and Villapiano, two of the leaders, would be traded. The beginning of free agency, where players could change teams every few years, was just down the road.

The days of the Raiders turning up for training camp early were over.

And while the final season was a downer when it ended and he called it quits, Madden walked away at the top. In a ten-year career, with 103 wins and a regular-season winning percentage of .763—better than the immortal Lombardi, whose winning percentage in ten years was .738.

Looking back today, how good were they? The Stabler-Biletnikoff-Upshaw-Tatum Raiders?

Madden paused before answering with a small smile: "You take whoever you want, then, and I'll play you." As in, "Choose the best players ever, anyone you can think of . . . and we'll beat you."

★ ★ ★

But he hadn't decided to leave the sideline because he was on top statistically. He also wanted to move on with his life and try something new. He knew there were new things to achieve in his life.

As he often says, if it's a game, then it should be fun. When it becomes too intense, it's not a game anymore. It was time to get back to the business of his life. He was forty-two, an age at which most people who wanted to be head coaches were waiting in line, when he decided to walk away.

Now, what to do next? At first, he thought, I'll get to finally spend some time with the wife and the kids. But that wasn't going to work. The Maddens had bought land up in the Altamont Pass and started a vineyard—Madden Ranch Vineyard—which occupied Virginia's time and energy. His kids had their own after-school friends. He agreed to help a friend who had a real estate office, but standing in line in some government office to get a permit to build some building convinced him that real estate was not going to be part of his future.

It was time to be a little less serious.

CHAPTER 10

IN 1978, TELEVISION COMMERCIALS aimed at sports fans were pretty boring. The Super Bowl commercials weren't any different from preseason-game commercials. They weren't very creative.

Budweiser beer's biggest commercial that year featured a couple coming home from work and unwinding with cans of Bud.

Then the ad agency for Miller, Bud's main competitor, struck gold. McCann-Erickson Worldwide had come up with a brilliant formula: getting former athletes and coaches to sell Miller Lite. But not the most famous figures—some of the most entertaining.

They brought in a few well-known guys—Billy Martin, the fiery Yankees manager, and Red Auerbach, the iconic Boston Celtic coach and general manager. They brought in some fringe sportsfolk, too, like Milwaukee Brewers broadcaster Bob Uecker and bench-riding baseball player Marv Throneberry. A couple of Madden's former players, defensive linemen Ben Davidson and Bubba Smith, were also part of the group.

The casting director, Marty Blackman, had his eye on the West Coast coach whose sidelines eruptions always had a sort of comical feel to them. So he called Madden in 1978, but the coach was sort of occupied.

Now, with Madden retired from the game, Blackman called again.

"I just want to relax," Madden said.

"But it's easy," said Blackman. "And the money is good."

When Blackman said Madden could do his audition in California, he agreed. Did Madden turn out to be a natural? Beyond Miller's wildest dreams.

"I remember when they told me, 'When you do

this commercial, more people are going to know you, and you're going to be in front of more people than ever.' I said, 'Are you kidding? I've been to Super Bowls.' This was nothing. But it turned out to really be something."

For his first commercial, Madden burst through a paper backdrop. The director thought it might be too violent, so they filmed a different ending. Fortunately, the Miller people went for the one where Madden burst through the paper.

"Along with my work at CBS," he wrote, "breaking through that paper for Miller Lite made me more famous than I ever was as a coach."

It wasn't just his sense of humor; it was his innate goofiness. This was a guy who, you could just tell, always saw nothing but the good in the situation, in people, in life.

The most memorable commercials were group commercials, sort of like an all-star game. You never knew who would be the featured characters in the group commercials, but Madden always was one of them.

The most famous was the "First Lite Beer Open,"

when Madden served as the announcer calling the madness as Uecker swings at a golf ball from ten feet underwater, Bubba Smith gets "a birdie" by accidentally hitting a bird, and Rodney Dangerfield scores a hole in one.

He enjoyed hanging with his new friends, and it wasn't work: Madden was having the time of his life. They all were. And it showed. "We were like regular people—that was the thing. That was real."

It's probably not coincidence that soon after he did his last one, the appeal of the commercials started to fade. The next round of characters couldn't carry the weight. And Madden had new places to go. His next career combined his love of the game and his natural vibe on camera.

But Madden and Miller Lite will apparently always live on. In October 2016, during a *Thursday Night Football* game, there it was: the original Madden-bursting-through-paper spot. Even three and a half decades later, Miller knew when it had a good thing.

CHAPTER 11

AFTER HIS RETIREMENT, Madden got a call from CBS exec Barry Frank: "Do you want to audition to be a television analyst?" It didn't sound like it was really up Madden's alley. He wanted to get into teaching.

For one thing, from a coach's point of view, he didn't hold the highest opinion of TV analysts. He'd gotten a little tired of hearing about something that the announcers had said about a play when they had little idea about what was actually happening.

"I didn't have a lot of respect for TV people at the time," Madden said. "They didn't prepare. They'd say things that weren't true. I'd hear on Monday about something some TV guy said, and they didn't even know if we had that play. That's why I first said no."

But Frank convinced him: "You ought to try it, John. . . . If you don't like it, at least you know you don't like it." So he auditioned for the heck of it. He got hired.

He hadn't really given it a lot of thought or preparation, so he asked Frank, "Now that I'm an announcer, what do I do?"

"Just talk to the people out there."

"But what people am I talking to out there? To grown-ups? To kids? To guys? To players? To ex-players? To people who know football? To people who don't know anything at all about football?"

"To all of them," Frank said.

And so he did. Like no one ever had, or ever will again.

Rudy Martzke, now retired from *USA Today,* was the dean of sports television critics for decades. Of Madden he says simply, "He was the best analyst of all time."

★ ★ ★

Madden chalks up some of his success (seventeen Emmys is a success, right?) to CBS's letting him develop. As a coach, he'd worked his way up step by step. In TV, he started with just four or five games in his first year.

"I had two or three years where I don't think anyone really watched, so you had a chance to become yourself before you got fired if they were going to fire you."

At first he was paired with such broadcasting legends as Lindsey Nelson and Jack Buck, who began to teach him the craft, although in the booth he didn't conform to the style of other color guys in the past. When the camera wasn't on him, he'd loosen his tie, take off his jacket, and flail his arms around, his voice rising excitedly. One time he almost knocked the glasses off booth-mate Gary Bender.

But the biggest difference between Madden and his peers was his way of getting from city to city: on the train.

Madden had always been kind of claustrophobic. As a kid, he'd sit at only one end of the dining room table or the other. Never in the middle. He'd sit in the aisle at movies.

As a coach, he'd had to overcome his airplane claustrophobia because there was no option. He couldn't travel without his team. But now, with a week between games, there was an alternative. Traveling from city to city on Amtrak gave him all the time in the world to study up on the upcoming game.

On his train rides, he would read notes on the players but never had to take notes of his own. His brain worked that way. Once he read, say, "The Eagles' quarterback is weak as a passer when he rolls to his left," it stuck, and he could summon it on the air.

But the real advantage Amtrak gave him in becoming a color analyst unlike any other was its spotty performance record. For one thing, Amtrak's long-distance trains ran only three times a week. On top of that, sometimes his train wouldn't even get into the city on the day it was supposed to: "Maybe you're hoping it gets there Wednesday, but you never know."

In 1969, at age thirty-two years, ten months,
John Madden became the youngest head
coach in pro football.

Madden was known for his wild sideline behavior.

John Madden cheers on his team.

Coach Madden and his Raiders celebrate after
winning their first Super Bowl.

Hall of Fame linebacker Ted Hendricks (*left*) and defensive lineman Charles Philyaw (*right*) carry their coach on their shoulders after the game.

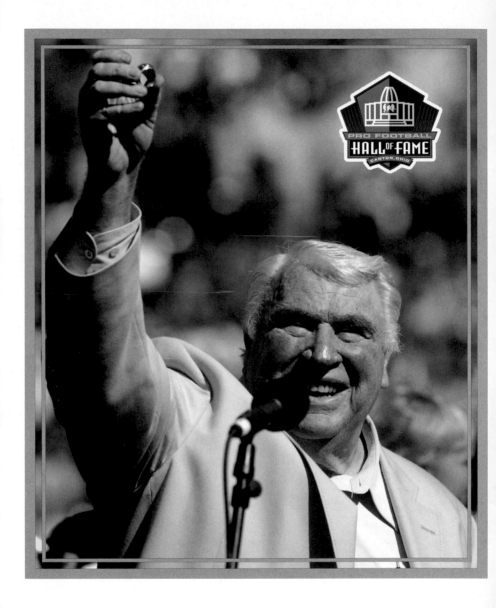

Madden receives his Hall of Fame ring,
one of the three icons—Bronze Bust, Gold Jacket,
and Ring of Excellence.

John Madden and Al Davis reveal
the bust of Madden at the
Pro Football Hall of Fame.

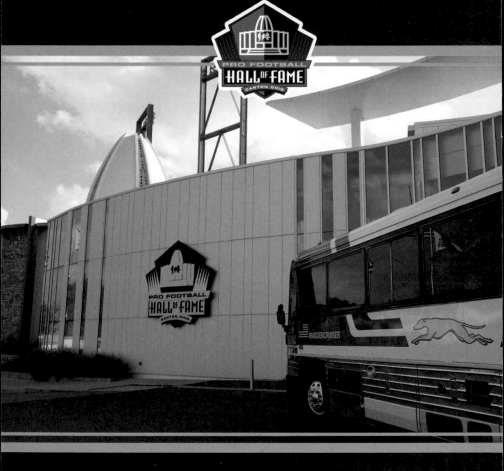

The famous Madden Cruiser is now in the

Pro Football Hall of Fame.

Amtrak had only a dozen national routes. Chicago to New York was easy: fifteen hours (and likely more) on a sleeper. But if he'd been in the booth for a game in Denver and his next assignment was in Dallas? He'd have to ride one train to Chicago, spend the night, and then catch another overnight train to Texas.

Then, after the game in Dallas, if he had to get back to, say, New York, he'd have to be driven to Meridien, Mississippi, to catch the train called the City of New Orleans.

Madden took to hopping the train a few days early, just in case, and so he often got into town days before the game. That meant he had a chance to prepare for games in a way that no other announcer before him had.

The teacher began to teach himself about a craft he'd never even considered taking on. He was able to watch practices and hang with the coaches.

"When I first started," Madden said, "the two announcers would fly into town on Saturday at noon or one, meet with the visiting PR guy for a half hour, then the home PR guy for another half hour, and the big question they asked was, 'How do you pronounce the names?'

"Then they'd go out and eat and drink and talk about what they were going to do for the opening. It was pretty simple. The announcers didn't know at the time they could talk to coaches and GMs and owners.

"So when I started getting there early, since I knew all the coaches, it was a chance to go to practice just by myself and talk to these guys. Because they were friends of mine, they'd give me their film to watch. I don't think anyone else was doing that.

"But I just sort of fell into it. I didn't do it for preparation. I was just hanging out. I watched film as a hobby anyway—it wasn't like, 'Shoot I have to go to work now.' It was, 'Hey, let's see what you're doing.'"

All of a sudden, this new analyst wasn't just stating the obvious about what had just happened down on the field.

He was telling the audiences *why* it happened. If the New York Giants were playing the Denver

Broncos, instead of saying, "The Giants' linebacker was out of position and missed the tackle," he could say, "The Broncos know that the Giants' linebackers like to split out wide, and that's why they're running inside. Now watch for the Giants to try to adjust, and the Broncos will start passing out of the backfield because the linebackers are playing the run."

★ ★ ★

Of course, the real appeal of the rails for someone mesmerized by other people's stories and lives was meeting people. Riding in a plane was the worst way to travel: going coast to coast in six hours and not meeting a single person in the three thousand miles!

"I'd been a lot of places as a coach, but I never saw anything," he said. "A hotel. A stadium. Another airplane. I was a lot of places, but I never saw anything."

He could hang in the dome car and chat with people from all over America, ask them questions about their lives. This was a social guy who didn't want to talk about himself. He was endlessly curious about others.

"I guess I could use the word *inquisitive* or *nosy*," he said of his interest in other people. "I just always wanted to know: 'What do *you* do?' It's always interesting, and it's always something so different from what you do.

"Sometimes it's something you've never heard before, maybe a guy getting out of jail, a professor. They would be equally interesting to me."

Amtrak's most celebrated rider would travel at least fifty thousand miles a year on the trains. He became so well known to the train crews that he got some special perks. Not favorable bedrooms or special service: food, of course.

Madden's regular daily meal routine in the dining car, where the crew would announce two or three times for seatings, would be pancakes for breakfast, cheeseburger and chili for lunch, and a steak for dinner.

(Madden train-dining tip number one: eat at the final seating, so you can linger as long as you want.)

But when the chefs whipped up a special meal for the crew, they'd let Madden in on a feast of oxtails and hot dogs, or red beans and rice, or sweet potato pie.

(Madden train-dining tip number two: be sure to wear something dark; eating on a swerving train can be a little messy.)

Just as fun as meeting fellow travelers was socializing with the conductors and porters. His conductor friend Elwood Best, riding from Denver east to his hometown of McCook, Nebraska, would phone ahead so that when the train stopped in McCook, Madden and Best would race across the street to the Speakeasy, where the hot-sausage sandwiches were waiting.

Then there was the time a freight train derailed in front of Madden's train, and during the delay, Madden hopped off and walked into the little town of Culbertson, Montana. It had one stoplight, about five hundred people, and a bar. That was Madden's destination.

"Set up the house," he shouted, like some cowboy who'd just found a gold mine in an old Western movie. "I'm buying!" And he did. Two hours later, he was out only twenty-five dollars, and when the train whistle blew, he walked back to the train.

All the guys at the bar felt as if they'd been in a real-life commercial.

CHAPTER 12

MAYBE ALL THE TIME he spent with average, normal people—the types of folk who aren't in a hurry or don't have the money for flying—had something to do with why he was immediately growing into the NFL's most popular analyst. He talked to the average person: a guy just like him.

He wasn't lecturing. He was talking to his friends. Everyone who loved football. Everyone who loved America's new best-loved sport.

"John was the common man," Robinson said. "He appealed to the blue-collar person in America. But he also appealed to the blue-collar guy's eighty-two-year-old grandmother. He had a great appeal to everybody."

"John spoke directly to the fans," Rudy Martzke said. "He had a way of explaining football to them that they didn't realize they didn't know. They were learning from him.

"On top of that, he had a wonderful delivery: upbeat, lively. There was humor at times, serious analysis at others."

Take his love of simple sound effects: "doink!" if a poor player fumbled a punt and the ball spun to the ground. Or maybe his most famous: "boom!" He'd use it, say, during a Redskins game when two of the huge "Hogs," the team's offensive linemen, teamed up to crush a defender: "You got six hundred and forty pounds of *guy* on you—boom!"

Why use five-dollar words when a one-syllable, little-kid sound conveys all you need it to? When you're talking about a 275-pound fullback nicknamed Meat and you say, *"All* fullbacks should be named Meat!" you're not talking to the stat geeks.

"He had a brilliant way of describing things," said Al Michaels, who would become his booth partner for *Monday Night Football* and NBC's *Football Night in America.* "He wasn't some oaf making guttural noises. People just loved listening to him.

"John is . . . John. He's not something that he's not, if that makes sense. He's just John Madden."

★ ★ ★

Until Madden's arrival, two-person broadcast teams stuck to a pretty limited formula: a veteran radio or TV guy who called the plays and a former player or veteran sportscaster who was supposed to bring analysis and "color" to the commentary. The second guy was usually commenting from the inside out, as if everyone knew about the game as well as he did.

But fans didn't know what they were missing until Madden was elevated to CBS's premier broadcast team to work with former New York Giant Pat Summerall. Summerall was a placekicker for three teams from 1952 to 1961.

Kickers have a lot of time to watch games, and when they're as bright as Summerall was, they learn a lot about their game. CBS used Summerall as an analyst for the first decade of his broadcasting career, when he was paired with just about every good play-by-play guy in the business.

But they thought that his skill set would be best used in the play-by-play role. They were right. In 1977, four years after his role had shifted, Summerall had been named the National Sportscaster of the Year.

Network executives first paired him with Madden for a Vikings game against the Tampa Bay Buccaneers in November 1979. Then, thinking they had found a broadcast team at the top of its game, they put Madden and Summerall together for the 1981 season . . . and the next twenty seasons after that.

★ ★ ★

Until then few fans cared who was calling a game on TV. But these two had a natural fit. There was chemistry in the broadcast booth and astute analysis from two men who knew the game inside and out. The key? Summerall never tried to rein Madden in when John felt like straying from the script, but he could also always bring him back to the business at hand with a word or two.

This gave Madden the confidence to say whatever he wanted, whether he was reviewing the tailgating food or the color of some new uniforms, because he knew Summerall would soon bring it all back into focus.

Matthew Shepatin, the author of *"Then Madden Said to Summerall . . . ,"* a collection of the best stories from the NFL's broadcast booths, simply called them "the all-time best."

From the start, Madden didn't worry about being "professional" and hiding an undisguisable love of the game. His commentary drew in both serious and casual fans.

In 1982, in his third season, his bosses gave him a new tool: "the chalkboard," which allowed him to draw (and scribble) on the screen as he broke down what had happened on the previous play.

It was an instant hit.

★ ★ ★

Summerall? His deep, bass voice grounded his words with confidence, all business . . . when he used them. Summerall was that wisest of announcers, knowing when to speak—and when not to.

When "Seventy-five yards . . . touchdown" was all you needed, why say more?

When Summerall spoke, people listened. It didn't matter that he was talking about football instead of finance, passes instead of politics.

"Pat was John Wayne and Walter Cronkite," Madden said, referring to the famed actor and the news broadcaster. "That's who he was."

It wasn't just their chemistry that made them the best. Viewers didn't know, but their spontaneous give-and-take was actually not spontaneous at all. Befitting everything Madden did, it was studied out.

"A lot of times, play-by-play guys can lead you into a corner, take you somewhere where you're not ready to go," Madden said. But with Summerall, that never happened. They had their routine down.

"Pat would finalize down and distance, then lay out, leave that hole for me. Then I'd watch the huddle, say something, and try to give it back to Pat." Summerall would describe the play, and then, after Madden gave his two cents (or two dollars), Summerall would have a brief synopsis.

"He was a genius with just a few words," Madden said. "He could take my rambling and answer in three or four words. And it wasn't him trying to help me be him. It was just Pat being Pat."

★ ★ ★

One of the highlights of Madden's CBS years was doing his buddy Robinson's Rams games. In 1986, the Rams were on a roll, winning six of their first nine games. Then they faced the Super Bowl champion Chicago Bears, with their legendary "Monsters of the Midway" defense, led by a defensive line that could pretty much handle any offensive line in the game.

"I can remember what he said at dinner the night before," Robinson recalled. "He said, 'I've got some advice for you. You're not going to score. In fact, you're not even going to get a first down. So just try to get back to the line of scrimmage.'"

The Rams won, 20–17.

★ ★ ★

Although his CBS booth became his classroom, Madden the teacher was still looking for a way to return to an actual classroom. So in the early eighties, he got a new gig at the University of California–Berkeley teaching . . . what else? Football.

His course, taught in the Education Department, was open to men and women. Always curious, Madden put together a class that might teach not only the students but also him. He had a feeling that people didn't really know much about football, at least not as much as they thought they did. He wanted to teach it as he'd teach a science or a skill.

"Men bluff that they do and try to bluff women. So I thought I'd start at zero and see how far they'd go. I'd start the class with, 'No one knows anything.' I'd start with the basics of the basics. Then I'd get deeper and deeper and deeper and deeper and deeper and deeper. Then I'd test them to see at what point I'd lose them."

The textbook? He wrote it himself.

CHAPTER 13

LIKE A LOT OF HISTORIC MOMENTS, when it happened, on board Amtrak's California Zephyr, no one noticed (except maybe one of Madden's conductor pals).

It was just a guy getting on a train in Denver in 1984 to meet another guy—John Madden—in the dining car to talk about an idea he had about a video game.

"He was waiting in the dining car," Trip Hawkins said, who is half of the team that created *Madden NFL,* the most successful sports video game in history. "He was a celebrity passenger, so Madden could hang in the dining car even when it was closed. We talked all day, into the evening, and across the rest of the country."

As an undergraduate at Harvard, Hawkins (unlike his new friend and business partner) had always taken his studies pretty seriously. He'd even designed his own undergrad major: Strategy and Applied Game Theory. But he'd also loved the game of football from childhood on.

"When I was a kid," he said, "I had my own transistor radio, and it was also the golden age of television, and I fell in love with football and baseball," he said. "The strategies of those two sports appealed to me."

But it was football's strategies that fascinated him most. He'd been a Kansas City Chiefs fan as a kid, when they were in their glory years under coach Hank Stram, winning Super Bowl IV. He'd even tried, as a kid, to pitch a board game to Chiefs owner Lamar Hunt. It didn't fly.

A self-described "student of football," Hawkins had also played and loved the game, as a wide receiver and defensive back on his high school team, then defensive back at Harvard as a freshman. Then Hawkins left the field and found his way up to, yes, Harvard Stadium's broadcast booth, where he could see the game unfold beneath him. Like Madden, he'd gone from playing the game to watching it before he decided that gaming was his future.

So he traveled west to Northern California and earned an MBA from Stanford. He knew he'd find a way to combine his love of gaming with his love of sports: "I thought, 'Wouldn't it be great to be able to simulate some of these powerful experiences adults have managing and coaching a professional team?'"

In the early 1980s, the video game universe was just waking up. Basic puzzle games like *Tetris* and *Super Mario Bros.* were fighting for market share with war games like *Gauntlet* and *Commando*.

Hawkins, working for Apple along with a crowd of other techies who'd found their way to Silicon Valley in its beginnings, wanted to design a football game that wasn't just fuzzy low-resolution figures of players butting heads and throwing a little football.

So he founded a gaming company called Electronic Arts, with the idea of developing all kinds of games. The football game Trip was thinking of creating had to be accurate. It had to involve strategy. It had to allow the gamer to play the role of coach.

But to design it, he needed a partner who knew everything about the game, whose name would bring cred. Whose expertise was, well, at the expert level.

"Very quickly I realized I wanted John Madden," Hawkins said. "By that time [1984], he was an American hero. He was so media-genic that he'd already become a media star. He appeals to men, to women, to kids. To all kinds of people whether they understood football or not.

"He's an incredibly smart man—and a no-bull guy. When you work with him, you find out that that persona on the air is a brilliant invention. He's a genius. It was easy for me to understand why he'd been so successful."

★ ★ ★

When Hawkins first approached Madden, John was interested, but not because he wanted his name to be on a game that people would play just for fun.

It was Madden the teacher who was immediately hooked on the idea.

"Trip was thinking about a *game* game," Madden said. "I was thinking about it as a teaching tool. The first thing I said to him was, 'I'm not going to do it unless there are twenty-two men on the field. I want linemen, I want stunts. I want the whole thing.'"

In those days, there weren't many sports games. When *John Madden Football* began selling well in 2001, the only sports video game that was even semipopular was a boxing game where two badly animated guys slugged it out.

Madden wanted his game to break some ground.

"When we started, I figured you could just put my plays in—some of the plays I taught in college—program them against the other team's defense, and then run the play on the computer, and then get percentages of success and everything.

"I thought using a computer could put you way ahead. It'd be a great coaching tool for high school, then maybe college, and even the pros."

About the same time, Hawkins approached two

other coaching legends to develop basketball and baseball games—Madden's Miller Lite buddy, Celtics legend Red Auerbach, and Baltimore Orioles manager Earl Weaver—but for various reasons, those games never happened. For sure, Hawkins's heart was in the football project: EA was really just "a means to an end," to come up with a football video game unlike any other, Hawkins said.

Madden and Hawkins stuck with it. And stuck. And stuck. Within a couple of years, the staff at EA had a nickname for the project: Trip's Folly.

The first version took three years, partly because the technology and programming were so new and difficult. But it was also because they designed the plays for the first games as they rode the trains.

Picture this: Two guys are sitting at a table up in the dome car as the cross-country train known as the California Zephyr winds its way through the beautiful snow-covered Front Range of the Rocky Mountains. Passengers sipping their drinks enjoy views of snowy pines and elk romping through the drifts at ten thousand feet.

But the two men aren't watching the scenery.

They're bent over a big piece of butcher paper laid out on the table. The big guy is drawing a football play. The other guy is nodding, asking questions and making suggestions. When he finishes, the big guy rolls up the piece of paper with the play on it. Then he draws another. And another.

Some time later, the other guy takes the papers back to his bedroom. When he debarks in Oakland, he takes them down to Silicon Valley.

That was the birth of the first game. "It was just me," Madden said, laughing and throwing out his arms in delight, "drawing plays on paper!"

Kind of like starting a fire with two sticks a few years before lighters are invented, right? Today, plays are designed by computers that have downloaded every play of the previous NFL season.

John Madden Football became *Madden NFL*, and it has taken its own place in the gaming Hall of Fame. It's generated more than four billion dollars in revenue and sold one hundred million copies. It's become the most popular sports video game in history.

The key to the game's popularity is Madden's

insistence that every new edition have new features. Players' stats are updated. New plays are added that reflect trends in the real game. Madden adds his own tweaks. He stays on top of everything from the rules regarding helmet-to-helmet hits to the climate of the stadium . . . not to mention the athletes themselves.

Another reason people keep buying, year in and year out, is free agency. In 1988, players weren't moving around from team to team. Now, starting rosters change every year. When Peyton Manning went from Indianapolis to Denver, you had to buy a new version of the game.

The year the game gained popularity was, probably not coincidentally, the first year that a picture of Madden was not on the cover. EA and Madden had decided to start putting a player on the cover. And not just any player, but players Madden admired—All-Madden Team guys.

Madden NFL was twenty-second and twenty-seventh in all categories the next two years.

One thing neither Madden nor Hawkins saw happening in the future was their game's popularity with actual NFL players. One former player esti-mates that half the NFL players play the game, often against old-time players they grew up watch-ing themselves.

A recent trend among some actual active NFL players is playing *Madden NFL* to heighten their own understanding of their own game. "To many players," wrote Ebenezer Samuel of the *New York Daily News*, "the game is now viewed as a solid test for football IQ. It's the football equivalent of the bonus-point take-home quiz from your favorite high school teacher."

"I played *Madden* the other day, and it's not just picking run plays anymore," said NFL quarterback Bryce Petty. "It's like, 'Oh, they've got an under front [on defense].' You start picking up things differently. That's exciting for me."

"I'm not gonna base my progress as an NFL player on *Madden*," lineman Weston Richburg said, "but playing football for the league . . . it has changed the way I play *Madden*. It's actually made it more fun, kind of more strategic."

Well, why wouldn't *Madden NFL* be played by

the real athletes? After all, as Hawkins explained, "there's no question that a whole lot of professional players have grown up learning about the game from the game. That actually happened."

Marketing-wise, sales are boosted by the wide and diverse demographics the game appeals to. Techies love it. Football-playing kids love it. Urban kids love it, suburban kids love it, and rural kids love it.

"And the guy who started playing at ten," Madden said, "is still playing at thirty."

And those real-life players are often obsessed with the *Madden* versions of themselves. Start with the receiver who kept looking over his shoulder as he raced downfield for a touchdown because his speed rating on *Madden* wasn't high, so he thought he was slow. "He said, 'I was watching *Madden,* and my speed on *Madden* was slow, and I knew the guy behind me runs faster. I knew he was going to catch me!'" Madden said, laughing. "He thought the speed he really had wasn't his real speed. It was his EA speed!"

Or how about the day that the great kick returner Devin Hester retired in 2017? Instead of using statistics from games to illustrate how great he was, social media networks posted graphics saying he was the only person to ever score one hundred for speed on *Madden*.

★ ★ ★

"When we first started, we wanted to make the game look like the NFL game," Madden said. "Then a few years ago, David Hill, the president of Fox Sports, said, 'We want our TV broadcast to look like this video game.' I thought, 'Holy smokes! We've come full circle!'"

In the 2017 season, the NFL took its imitation even further. An unexpected fog filled Gillette Stadium during a Patriots game against the Atlanta Falcons, and the TV cameras couldn't penetrate it. So NBC used its SkyCam, a computer-controlled camera that rides a kind of tightrope.

The result? The game unfolded for viewers just the way *Madden NFL* does.

There was so much positive feedback that three

weeks later, NBC actually used SkyCam as its live play-by-play camera for a Thursday night game between the Tennessee Titans and the Steelers.

But the game's co-inventor is the first to admit that he never thought any of this would happen.

"I don't know that anyone else did, either," he said. "No one knew what was going to happen. To say I knew what was going to happen twenty years later . . . When it happens this big, there has to be some luck."

But that luck was enhanced by the man: a teacher who, with the help of a Harvard guy and fellow lover of the game, found a new way to keep teaching the sport he loves.

CHAPTER 14

FOR EIGHT YEARS, Madden gladly put up with the inconvenience of the trains. It was cool to fall asleep to the rocking of the train car and hang with the conductors.

Then, one day in 1987, CBS told Madden that it wanted to film a spot featuring Madden playing pool with two famous pool players, Willie Mosconi and Minnesota Fats, in Las Vegas. To do that, he had to get from Atlanta to Philadelphia for the next week's game. But there was no way the trains could get him out to Vegas and back in time.

"Let's rent you a private bus," said CBS's Terry O'Neil, a bus "like entertainers use."

No one knew that O'Neil's quick-fix solution to a one-time problem would result in one of the most celebrated chapters in NFL lore, not to mention the most famous bus in American history: the birth of the Madden Cruiser.

A little background: When Madden's wife was earning her master's degree, she studied John Steinbeck, the legendary West Coast writer who set his best stories in the Monterey Peninsula, south of San Francisco.

That was Madden land: Northern California.

Steinbeck's *Travels with Charley* was the author's chronicle of a road trip all around America with his poodle Charley. He stopped in small towns and learned what the people of America were all about and what mattered to them.

When Madden picked it up and read it, the book struck a chord with him. He kept the thought in the back of his head: How cool would it be to travel America and stop wherever and whenever you wanted to talk to farmers and fishermen?

Remember Madden said that as a coach he "never saw anything." Then he saw a lot of things—but only where the train went. How cool would it be for him to now go anywhere in America and talk to anyone? On the unfanciest way of traveling in America?

His first experience with bus travel, though, was pretty fancy.

CBS had rented country-music queen Dolly Parton's ride. Dolly's bus was decked out for pure luxury.

It was a sign of things to come.

★ ★ ★

Rudy Martzke was an award-winning sports media columnist for *USA Today* for more than twenty years. He was the first writer to ever accompany Madden on a cross-country train trip. And he was the only writer to meet Madden at his apartment in the fabled Dakota apartment building in New York before they got on the train.

The Dakota was the first building on the Upper West Side of Manhattan, built in 1880, and ever since, it's been the most storied residence in the city, home to artists as diverse as John Lennon and Judy Garland and Leonard Bernstein.

But Madden didn't spend a lot of time chatting with his neighbors. He hadn't chosen the apartment because it was an A-list celebrity haunt. He'd chosen it because it had nice apartments, and if he had to have a New York address because of his full-time work for CBS, the Dakota was pretty cool.

But no, he didn't want to hang with other celebrities. When he was in the Dakota, he preferred to hang with the doormen, Joe and José. Better yet, he preferred to walk across Central Park West, just outside Central Park, and watch the crowd—and, as always, satisfy his curiosity about their lives.

"He'd sit on a bench and look at people as they went by," Robinson said. "He'd say to me, 'Hey, I was sitting in the park, and I saw this guy,' and they'd ended up talking.

"It could be Paul Simon, who lived up somewhere nearby, or somebody eccentric. That's who John was really interested in talking to. With John, it wasn't that thing where some guy is coming over and you turn your back and you hope he doesn't ask you for a dollar.

"John would say, 'Hey, come on over here!'"

★ ★ ★

After meeting Madden at his apartment in the Dakota and cabbing it to Penn Station, Martzke and Madden rode overnight on the Lake Shore Limited before they transferred to the Southwest Chief to travel to the Rose Bowl in Pasadena, California, for the Giants-Broncos Super Bowl. "See you in the observation car," Madden told Martzke as they boarded and headed for their respective sleeping quarters.

Riding on the Gannett Company's dime, of course, Martzke was on a budget and had the smallest compartment available, which included its own toilet.

"The only time I was ever on a train was as a little kid," Martzke said, "so I open the toilet lid and peed. Then I can't find a button to flush it. I fumble around and see a cord, so I pull it—and the shower comes on! So now I stumble backward and out the door into the hallway—just as John is coming down the aisle."

But the rest of the ride was a blast, Martzke remembers. Watching the country roll by, Madden would provide a running commentary on each state's characteristics and its people. He would happily mingle with other riders, finding out about their lives.

Meanwhile, Martzke filed daily columns about being on the train with America's most famous railroad rider. One of them quoted Madden talking about how the trains were getting inconvenient, scheduling-wise. He told Martzke he was thinking about getting a bus. Martzke filed the column.

Meantime, when PBS correspondent Elizabeth Brackett boarded the train in Chicago to interview Madden, he told her the same thing.

Her interview ran on TV the Friday before the game. And it so happened that meanwhile, in a motel in Arizona, a guy named George Gravley, the public relations director for Greyhound, saw the segment and made a note to himself.

The next day, he was on a flight with the chairman of the board of Greyhound, which was negotiating with its workers for a new labor contract. Fred G. Currey, Greyhound's CEO, was reading *USA Today*'s sports section, with Martzke's column . . . and right then and there, they decided that they'd make Madden an offer: a free bus.

Greyhound's pitch? He'd have his own bus-yacht. . . . All Madden had to do was give motivational speeches to Greyhound employees on his trips from city to city. After three years, he could have the bus free and clear.

"No commercials?" Madden asked his agent. "No ads?"

Nope. Just talk to the workers.

And that's how Madden got a bus that cost half a million dollars in return for his true talent: coaching and teaching.

No way the guy who'd loved *Travels with Charley* for thirty years would turn down that offer.

The next step was to have an audition for the prestigious position of Madden Cruiser driver. Greyhound brought in eight of its best drivers from around the country. They took a written test, took a drive on the freeway, drove around cones in the Coliseum parking lot, and interviewed with Madden.

The winner was Willie Yarbrough of Whittier, California, a driver for two decades on Greyhound's Los Angeles–Sacramento route. "He always had a smile on his face and a bounce in his walk," Madden said. Yarbrough quickly became the subject of newspaper stories himself.

On the side of the bus, Greyhound wanted to paint a portrait of Madden bursting through a window, like the Miller Lite thing, but Madden refused. He settled for the words *Madden Cruiser* up on the curving sides of the roof—visible to truckers, who would constantly call him on their CB radios and chat.

★ ★ ★

And so, in the fall of 1987 the blue-collar American announcer was now riding the average American's way of riding: the bus.

But what a bus.

Start with the queen-size, ultrafirm bed, which took up the rear third of the bus. It was almost as wide as the bus itself.

Extra-sized bathroom, tiled shower.

Up front? Blue leather chairs. Upholstered couch.

The dining area was extra big, and the table where he ate had places for poker chips in each corner . . . as well as six extra inches of stomach room.

Two twenty-inch color TVs. Thermostat kept at fifty-nine degrees.

The Madden Cruiser quickly became a national attraction, no matter where it was parked. Fans wanted to go inside. Packers coach Forrest Gregg wanted to go inside. Steelers owner Art Rooney wanted a tour.

And, of course, his pal Willie Nelson had to have a tour, to see if Madden's bus was cooler than his.

But it wasn't a king's carriage. It belonged to a really humble guy. And when he got off the Madden Cruiser, the man who'd recently won his fourth Emmy wanted to hang with America's people, not its stars. John Madden the announcer had become something more: John Madden the American wanderer, lover of road food, and all-around American folk hero. He took to America's roads and became the modern version of his favorite American writer.

"You want to meet everybody," he said. "The thing is, I'm always more interested in what they do than talking about myself. I really wondered why people did what they did or lived where they lived.

"So you'd see a farmhouse and you'd think, 'What do they know? What do they do? How do they think? What's important to them? Where do they shop? How can you live out here in the middle of nowhere?'

"Then you find out they couldn't live anywhere else. Like one time I was talking to a dairy farmer from Wisconsin. He'd never had a vacation. I said, 'Why don't you take some time off?' He looks at me and says, 'The cows have to be milked every day. You can't tell a cow, I'm going to take off for two weeks, and milk yourself.'"

The bus also allowed him to stay in touch with

his major passion: sports. Any time they'd be driving at night and Madden spotted a lighted field, he'd tell the driver to pull over.

Whether it was a nighttime local softball-league game or a high school football practice, he said, "I couldn't pass up the game."

Or the food, when he was able to both eat and catch the Monday night game at the same time. He hated not being able to see every *Monday Night Football* game.

One night in Sidney, Nebraska, the bus stopped at a Tastee Freez to watch the Monday night game on a black-and-white TV. Madden was pretty much alone until someone called the local high school coaches.

The boys' basketball team showed up in uniform (the coach had ended practice early), and the football coach showed up with his wife.

Then, one Monday night in October 1987, with the bus heading west about a hundred miles east of El Paso, when the Browns-Rams game was about to start, Madden was exceptionally eager to watch because the Browns were playoff-bound.

But there was no TV reception out there, fifty miles north of the Mexican border on I-10 West.

So Willie pulled into Van Horn, Texas (population 2,000), where they saw an inviting sign: MEXICAN FOOD. TV ROOM.

It was the perfect Mexican place: great food, a TV tuned to the game. Not only that, it got better: the proprietor of Chuy's, Jesus (Chuy) Uranga, noticed that when Madden ordered, he definitely knew his Mexican food, so Uranga offered him some of his wife's special tortillas that she'd just cooked.

Uranga and Madden watched the first half. By the time the Madden Cruiser got back on the interstate and a little closer to El Paso, they were able to get the game on the bus.

The Browns won, 30–17.

★ ★ ★

There were too many off-the-radar restaurants to remember, but Madden couldn't ever forget the time they were rolling southbound along I-65 on their way to a New Orleans Saints game and spotted a sign in Atmore, Alabama: CREEK FAMILY RESTAU-RANT, owned by the Creek Confederacy.

It was Madden's kind of place. He didn't know what the gray building next door was, but the buffet was everything a road warrior could want: fried chicken, smoked sausage, catfish, roast beef, spaghetti, vegetables, and corn bread.

"The bus would be driving down the middle of some road somewhere," Robinson said, "and someone would say, 'Let's go there.'

"'Nope,' John would say. John would find some of the worst places you could ever find. If the place was worn down and had lots of beat-up cars outside, we'd stop. That's where he was comfortable."

One time, the bus stopped in Beaver Crossing, Nebraska (population 403), so that Madden could use the pay phone. Two days later, this was the headline of a story in the *Omaha World-Herald:* MADDEN STOPS TO USE THE PHONE.

It wasn't just the food that Madden loved about being on the backroads of America. The guy who was curious about everything liked to look at the scenery, too. He'd keep track of the wildflowers from the book his son had given him, *Wildflowers Across America*.

"That's spotted knapweed," he'd say to a riding guest.

Whether it was the people, the food, or the plants that made his ride so much fun, there's no question that, at the end of the day—or the end of the voyage—America's favorite football commentator was glad he'd made the trip.

"You get out there, and it makes you feel better about America," he said. "The thing works."

Robinson, it should be noted, never took another ride: "He had this huge bed, and I had to sleep in a chair. Never again."

★ ★ ★

Rudy Martzke didn't mind sleeping upright on his three trips on the bus. Each one was an adventure.

On the first, when they pulled up in front of a Mexican place in Arkansas and Martzke started to head inside, Madden stopped him. "Where you going? We exercise first!"

"What's the exercise?"

"First, we have to do a lap."

"Of what?"

"Around the bus."

On the next trip, Madden took his weight-watching seriously. He'd picked up a blender and was making healthy smoothies. At a gas station, Martzke made the mistake of buying a bag of caramel corn. He was talking to his wife, Mouse, on a pay phone when Madden took the phone.

"Is this Mouse? I am really upset at your husband."

"What for?" said Mouse.

"He brought caramel corn onto the bus."

"He had to feign anger," Martzke said. "He wasn't very good at it."

★ ★ ★

The bus also allowed Madden to mingle with his favorite people in the football community: the fans out in the parking lots.

Of course, this also allowed him to eat, and eat

well. All the tailgaters wanted him to sample their feasts after he'd parked the bus and started to walk into each stadium. His love of tailgating feasts became a meme on the telecasts: during a down moment, he'd narrate while the camera showed someone cooking bratwurst or wings.

"Tailgate people . . . they have the most fun at the game," Madden said. "They are the friendliest people. They want to share. 'Here, try this,' they'll say."

And since what they wanted him to try was delicious food, who was he to turn down their generosity? Especially in his three favorite parking lots: Kansas City, Buffalo, and Green Bay?

It wasn't just Kansas City's world-famous barbecue that made it a tailgating capital for Madden. It was because the lot and stadium were beneath a hill, so when the bus came down to the parking lot, it entered into a haze of sweet barbecue smoke.

Buffalo? "One thing about cold weather," he said, "there's a double dip there. There's the food, but there is also the fire there to keep you warm. You tend to get more cooks in the stew."

Green Bay? Because of the grilled bratwurst and sausages. And NFL tradition.

Madden became so famous as a tailgate expert that he wrote a book of tailgating recipes.

★ ★ ★

One meal in particular became Madden's culinary calling card. The turducken was the Frankenstein monster of game birds.

The turducken origin story, like a lot of good food stories, begins near New Orleans, in Maurice, Louisiana, west of the city. One day, goes the tale, a farmer walked into Hebert's Specialty Meats in Maurice and asked if the butcher could make one meal out of a duck, a chicken, and a turkey.

So the butcher, Glenn Mistich, sewed a deboned duck inside a deboned chicken inside a deboned turkey with special dressings in between. The turducken was born!

Now, it so happened that his shop advertised on a local radio station, pitching the specialty, and one day before Madden was coming to town for a Saints game, an announcer suggested they ought to get a turducken into the hands of the man. That's how famous Madden had become as a foodie. Mistich and the radio guy got to the Saints' PR people, who took it up to the booth.

"I didn't have any plates or silverware or anything," Madden said, "and I just started eating it with my hands." Legend has it that when Saints owner Tom Benson stopped by the booth and shook Madden's hand, there was kind of an awkward moment because Madden didn't want to get the bird fat on the owner's hands.

But Madden liked the dish so well he asked the butcher to send him one in California. The next year, the Thanksgiving turducken food-sharing tradition began. That was the season that, after the Thanksgiving game he'd done with Summerall, he and the producers decided to have him name a Madden MVP of the game.

Immortal lineman Reggie White won the honors, walked over to a table on the field that held the turducken, ripped off a leg, and eagerly chomped it on national television. A tradition was born.

But then, Madden thought, what if next year's MVP wasn't just one guy? What if it were, say, the whole offensive line? You couldn't have the center tearing into his leg while the other four three-hundred-pounders fought over the second leg. (With Madden, the old tackle, doing the selecting of the MVP, this was a definite possibility.)

"So then we started 'creating' turkeys with more legs," he said. "We made four-legged turkeys, six-legged turkeys, eight-legged turkeys."

So that meant that on any given Thursday morning, as it pulled into the Thanksgiving Day city, the Madden Cruiser would be carrying five or six turkeys and a turducken or two for good measure. He'd park the bus next to the production trucks, lay out a turkey buffet, and let the workers from the network have their own feast.

Then, Madden thought, since he was always calling the Thanksgiving game on the road, and the network's crew was working away from home on Thanksgiving, the guys laying wire and taping cables from the truck to the booth and doing all the blue-collar work, wouldn't this be a great way to feed them?

So basically, from the game's MVP down to the kid laying tape in the parking lot, everyone got fed.

By the time the bus pulled out for the next town, nothing was left but a lot of turkey bones.

The Madden turducken gained even more fame when that Frankenstein monster of a meal became the official dish of the All-Madden Team.

CHAPTER 15

IT'S PRETTY FITTING, if you believe in friendships, that the legendary All-Madden Team, his celebration of the tough, muddy players who played the game with reckless abandon, wasn't even his idea. It was his pal John Robinson, then the head coach of the Rams, who launched the team.

One day, as they were eating, Robinson suggested that there should be an all-star team that celebrated the NFL players who didn't get enough recognition: the tough, unknown linemen, and the fullbacks who threw blasting blocks, and the special-teams guys who flew down the field at full speed without regard for personal safety.

These guys didn't get impressive stats, so they didn't get to be "stars," as far as the fans' thinking went. But these were the very kinds of players that Madden and Robinson had loved as a kid.

"'Yeah,' I said," Madden recalled. "'Then we could go back to what it was like when we were kids, when we pretended to be our favorite players. We could have Lawrence Taylor here, another guy there. All the positions. We could have a dinner!'"

It was just two pals shooting the breeze over a casual lunch at work.

What they didn't know was that CBS Sports executive producer Terry O'Neil had overheard their conversation.

★ ★ ★

The timing was perfect. In 1984, no one had yet figured out what programming to put on TV the Sunday between the championship games and the Super Bowl, two weeks later.

A light went on over O'Neil's head: this idea, he thought, could be a great TV show for the network.

The next time Madden heard about the All-Madden Team was on the air.

"We're doing a game," he said, "and I see a promo: 'Coming up in two weeks: the All-Madden Team.' I guess Terry thought it was a good idea, or thought we wanted to do it, or maybe both."

He had no idea that Robinson's idea was going to become real. But looking back, it made a lot of sense.

"They have so much content now; there'd be no place for something like that. But back then, it was an open page we could write anything in. And that's what we did."

People liked it because, like everything Madden touched when it was about the game he loved, the All-Madden Team celebrated the heart of the game, instead of the glamour.

The announcing of the All-Madden Team became must-see TV—especially for the friends and family of the guys who hoped they'd finally get their moment in the sun because they played football the Madden way: for the average fan who appreciated the workers in the trenches. Like, for instance, Stan Brock.

Brock, a captain as an offensive lineman at Colorado, was picked in the first round of the 1980 draft by the then-woeful New Orleans Saints. In Brock's first year, the Saints lost fifteen of sixteen games. In his first three years, they won nine games total. They didn't break .500 until his eighth year.

Brock was a Saints captain, but the star-makers didn't pay a lot of attention, because those Saints never had an All-Pro running back. Linemen don't get noticed without star runners behind them.

That's why, one day after the 1990 season—yet another year in which the "Ain'ts" hadn't qualified for the playoffs—Brock and his dad were wandering through a fishing-and-hunting store when his dad saw the Madden team being announced on a TV screen.

"Think you'll make it?" asked his dad.

Brock shook his head: "They would have let me know."

But when they drove back to his folks' place, his mom was waiting out front: "You made the All-Madden Team! You made the All-Madden Team!"

"One of the great awards I've ever gotten," he says now. "I mean, for an offensive lineman to be chosen by Coach Madden was special. Even the All-Pro and Pro Bowl are voted on by your opponents, and there can be a lot of politics in that. It was never my job to have my opponent like me. So knowing that Coach Madden had the ultimate input?"

It's been almost thirty years since that day. That Brock still calls him "Coach" shows the personal relationship the players felt with Madden and the All-Madden Team.

"I think it was really good for the game," Brock said. "Here's a guy who was really successful as a coach, and everyone loved him as an announcer because he just talked about the offensive linemen of the world. Just the guys who grab their lunch bucket, do their jobs. No giant paychecks, no real glory. They just did it for the love of the job.

"Look at America today. He was talking to the worker bees of America who appreciate offensive linemen, and I know that offensive linemen appreciate the guys who get their hands dirty and work for a living . . . and come home to [run] around in the backyard with their kids.

"I think that's what he represented to the country.

For him to pick this team, everyone was anxious and excited—the players *and* the fans. Who's going to be named this year? The guys we can relate to? They might not have the highest stats, but they lined up and they went to work."

For the guys like Brock, there were perks: the annual banquet, where, if he couldn't make it, he'd weigh in by remote camera.

"It became pretty damned big," Madden said. "It was fun."

It was a great era. Trouble is, when Madden left the booth, the All-Madden Team faded into history. Today, there are awards for just about everything. But none for just playing your heart out.

CHAPTER 16

IN 1994, FOX WON the rights to broadcast NFC games and announced that Madden and Summerall would be its top team. They would call three more Super Bowls before Summerall announced in 2002 that he would be retiring. Madden moved over to join Al Michaels in the *Monday Night Football* booth.

★ AL MICHAELS ★

At the 1980 Winter Olympics in Lake Placid, New York, the US ice hockey team beat the Soviet Union, 3–2, in the medal round, on its way to win the gold. According to *Sports Illustrated,* it was the most memorable sports moment of the twentieth century.

In the last seconds of the game, with the Americans about to defeat the mighty Soviets for the first time in two decades, ABC's play-by-play announcer gave us the most famous sports call ever: "Do you believe in miracles?" shouted Al Michaels. *"Yes!"*

Many years later, Michaels would be called "the dean of network play-by-play men." Before the 1980 Olympics, he wasn't a household name. It had been a long climb, all the way from childhood.

When other kids were learning their ABCs, five-year-old Michaels started pretending he was the announcer of games on the television in his parents' living room in Brooklyn, New York. A few years later, he would carry an old tape recorder that weighed as much as a bowling ball to the Brooklyn Dodgers games at Ebbets Field, calling the games into the microphone.

All that studying began to pay off. As a student at Arizona State University, he was the announcer for more than two hundred college games. Six years later, after announcing lots of sports at many levels, he landed the play-by-play job for the Cincinnati Reds in 1971, and when the Reds went to the World Series in 1972, he announced those broadcasts.

A few years later, ABC hired him to call national baseball games and the Olympics. Finally, in 1986, he landed in ABC's prestigious *Monday Night Football* booth.

ABC had taken a bold chance with pro football on a Monday night when it launched in 1970. But it paid off big-time when the broadcasting trio of Frank Gifford, Howard Cosell, and former Cowboys quarterback Don Meredith brought the game into living rooms around the nation. It was all as much showbiz as sports, growing a whole new crop of fans.

Michaels took over Gifford's play-by-play

role. ABC paired him with five different analysts, but none of them were able to make audiences smile. Then Madden came on board in 2002. The two men had talked a lot when Madden was a coach. Now, in the booth, Michaels and Madden clicked immediately. When the producer of their first game said, "Do you want to rehearse?" both said, "We don't have to."

There were as many laughs as there were football plays, and once again the Monday night game was must-see sports TV.

Four years later, the NFL broadcasting landscape shifted. *Monday Night Football* moved to cable, but NBC added a new Sunday night game. Madden and Michaels were its first announcers, with as much appeal as always.

When Madden called it quits four years later, Cris Collinsworth took over next to Michaels, and those two are still going strong.

Michaels's fame isn't just because he's an expert on all the sports he announces. It's because he always sounds like a fan watching the game along with the rest of us.

"If you script something," the most famous play-by-play announcer of sports once said, "if you plan something, it will sound that way."

★ ★ ★

When Michaels found out he was going to be paired with Madden, he had an idea it was going to work out because he remembered the first time he'd met the man, when Michaels was covering a Raiders game for NBC.

"We sat in his office," Michaels said, "and talked about *Travels with Charley*. He'd said he wanted to be able to live it out, Steinbeck's book. We talked about football about twenty-five percent of the time that day."

Summerall had first brought out Madden's talents as a commentator, as a former player working with a former coach. Michaels came from a different breed of announcers: men who had grown up dreaming of doing not the playing but the announcing. Now Madden was in the booth with a teacher who had never wanted to do anything but be a broadcaster.

With the pro at his side, Madden took it to the next level. By the end of this broadcasting episode, Madden had become an all-star.

Said Martzke: "He was the best of all time of any analyst."

★ ★ ★

In the new *Monday Night* booth, Madden and Michaels were a hit from the start.

"When they put us together," Michaels said, "I knew this was a can't-miss. To try to break it down as to why? I can't. From the start, we were just ourselves."

Before their first official game, calling the Hall of Fame Game in Canton, their producer suggested they call a game on a dummy camera for practice, to just prepare . . . "to roll the tape, sit in the studio, do some back-and-forth," Michaels said.

"John looked at me, and I said, 'I don't think we need it.'"

They knew they were ready, even if they'd never called a game together.

After the meeting, Madden said to Michaels, "I'm glad you said that."

"I think we both knew," Michaels said, "that it was going to work."

And it did, for the next seven years, four of them for ABC. Then, when ESPN took over the *Monday Night Football* broadcast, the pair moved over to NBC's new *Sunday Night Football* show, which debuted in 2006.

The network hadn't broadcast NFL football since 1998, and when it reentered the picture, it did so with a bang. The show was a whole new animal: studio talk, highlights of the day's games, and a full ninety minutes of entertaining pregame before the actual game rolled around.

Three years later, having worked for all four networks, and having spent three decades in those booths, Madden decided to call it quits.

"I'd had enough—that's it," he said. "When I do

something like that, I know there's no looking back. It was like when I stopped coaching.

"It wasn't like, 'I'll try retirement, and if it doesn't work, I'll come back.' No, when I leave, I'm gone. So with television I just thought, one day, *I'm done.* Never went back."

He loved his time in the booths. But even though a lot of people know him more for his broadcasting than his coaching, the experience wasn't on par.

"The number one thing is playing. That's number one. Nothing else beats playing. Then coaching comes second. Then broadcasting would be third.

"In playing, you win or lose. In broadcasting, you don't win or lose. You play to win. You coach to win."

CHAPTER 17

FOR ANYONE WHO EVER plays the pro game or prowls a sideline wearing a headset, grumbling at the refs and giving a backslap to the running back who just scored the touchdown as he runs off the field, it's the highest height:

The Hall of Fame.

It's not the reason you play or coach the game, but it's the ultimate honor.

It surprised no one that Madden was a finalist in his first eligible year, 1985. It surprised a lot of people when, the next year, his name had dropped off the list of finalists.

The year after that, Gene Upshaw got in on his

first year of eligibility. Madden wasn't a finalist. The year after, Fred Biletnikoff was ushered in. Madden wasn't a finalist that year. The year after that? Left tackle Art Shell got in. The year after that? Ted Hendricks. No mention of their coach.

Twenty years after that first nomination, his name still hadn't appeared again. "I don't know why," Madden said.

On paper, statistics-wise, if the forty-eight media voters were going strictly by numbers, it was hard to understand.

Don Shula, Chuck Noll, and Tom Landry, for instance, were inducted in their first eligible year even though each of their regular-season winning percentages (.676, .566 and .605, respectively) were far lower than Madden's. But Noll had four Super Bowls, Shula and Landry two.

Then again, Madden's division rival Hank Stram got in in 2003, and he'd won only one Super Bowl. His regular-season winning percentage was only .574.

More noticeably, Stram's teams won four division championships in seventeen years.

Madden's teams won seven in ten.

But here's something the other four had that Madden didn't: being seen by the media as the faces of their franchises. No one ever associated Noll's Steelers with anyone other than Chuck. Ditto for Landry and the Cowboys, Shula and the Dolphins, Stram with the Chiefs.

When those forty-eight writers and broadcasters had written about the great successes of those four teams, their readers and viewers were always hearing about those coaches.

★ ★ ★

When the media talked about the wildly successful Raiders of the seventies? It was always known as Al Davis's team. He'd become the larger-than-life face of the Raiders ever since he'd tried to wrest the commissionership of the merging leagues from incumbent Pete Rozelle.

Whether he was winning a Super Bowl ring or moving the team or suing the league, he was the Oakland Raiders. Madden was the man who won the ring in 1977, but in NFL lore and myth, he was Davis's employee.

Davis's name made the list of Hall of Fame finalists one year after Madden's, and appeared five more times before, in 1992, in his seventh year of being a finalist, he made it in.

The man who introduced him? John Madden. His speech was everything you'd expect from football's best-loved ambassador: he was the voice of all of us who love the game.

"I am not up here as John Madden introducing Al Davis," Madden said. "I'm up here as everyone. . . . Family, players, coaches, all you people, I represent you, all you fans."

When Davis took the podium to speak, he began by thanking Madden and then added, "John Madden will take his rightful place in the Hall of Fame in the very near future."

But Davis's induction didn't do anything to boost Madden's stock.

As the years went on, his being excluded wasn't a reason to gripe or moan. "After a while, you learn not to get involved," he said. "You stay uninvolved."

All he cared about, as he went about the business of broadcasting and working on the video game, was that he was still playing instead of working. And he was still playing in January 2006, when he and Michaels were set to call Super Bowl XL between the Steelers and the Seattle Seahawks in Detroit. But something had changed.

He'd finally been nominated as a finalist again, but this time in a different way: as a contributor. The founders of the Hall's eligibility rules had the foresight to know that there'd be people who'd be giants in the growth and development and legacy of the game who would never play or coach, and so they instituted a contributor category for "individuals who made outstanding contributions to professional football in capacities other than playing or coaching."

By now Madden's contributions to the game had gone way beyond his record on the field. From the broadcast booth, where, on this weekend, he was about to call his tenth Super Bowl, he'd sold the game to countless listeners who might not have been NFL fans but loved the way he reached men, women, boys, and girls.

Whether it was because of the fun of the All-Madden Team or just his friendly approach, Madden had become one of the best ambassadors the game had ever known. So he couldn't help wondering if he'd get a call from the Hall of Fame selection committee. But he knew the call always came around noon, and when one o'clock rolled around, he thought he'd been passed over again.

"They'd call you right away. I just thought, 'I didn't make it,'" he said. "[In the studio] on Saturday, the NFL Network was on TV, and Rich Eisen was on. My producer said, 'You want me to turn this off?'

"'Naw,' I said. 'Let's see who made it.' We're watching. They start off. Troy Aikman. That makes sense. Harry Carson. Sure.

"Then they say, 'John Madden.'

"I didn't expect it. . . . That's a knockout punch. I was just shocked."

"He had a phenomenal broadcasting career after having a phenomenal coaching career," Michaels said. "He had a Hall of Fame coaching career, and he had a Hall of Fame broadcasting career."

★ ★ ★

"It means everything," Madden said. "The Hall of Fame is where you want to be. That's the thing. Now you're in there with the best of all time. They can never take it away from you. You're going to be there forever...and ever and ever and ever and ever and ever and ever and ever."

The cool thing is that when Madden was introducing Davis, he wanted to talk to every inductee and every guy who'd already been inducted. Just as when he'd talked to every Pro Bowl player trying to find out what it took to win a Super Bowl, he loved talking to the all-stars in his profession.

Then he got to be one of them. And they blew him away.

"Once you're one of them, when you walk into a room, there's never not a place to sit.... The stories. Seeing these guys! Gale Sayers. Joe Perry. Bigger-than-life guys.

"It's much more than getting honored. It's a life. It's, you know, it's a very exclusive club, and you can't get in unless you earn your way in. There's no way to buy your way in. Then when you get there, you respect everyone there because you know they earned their way into it.

"The thing is, I think the long wait makes you appreciate it more. I don't know that anyone can appreciate it more than I did. If you get it, sometimes, I see these guys get it right off the bat, and to them it's a gig. Oh, I got to go to a dinner. No, man, it's the Hall of Fame! This isn't a dinner. It's the Hall of Fame!"

And a room full of busts.

"Yeah," Madden said, drawing on his goofy side. "I do think the busts talk to each other. They have to. When you really think about it, there has to be more than making a bust and putting it in a room forever. It has to be more than that."

Who's your bust talking to?

"All of them," he said.

If only we could hear that conversation.

CHAPTER 18

HE'S STILL PLAYING.

Every Sunday.

The playing field is housed in the headquarters of Goal Line Productions, Madden's office complex in Pleasanton, California, a pretty, peaceful village twenty-five miles east of downtown Oakland.

It's a little different from Madden's Lot, this place where the games happen on Sundays, but it's about as big.

It's a giant wall in a really large room that, once a week, is full of football. Taking up most of the wall are nine sixty-three-inch flat-screen TVs that surround the middle screen, which is nine by sixteen feet. Basically, it's a movie screen surrounded by smaller movie screens, and it is every football fan's ultimate dream.

He got the idea a long time ago, the first time he walked into a production truck and saw all those games being played around him. Someday, he thought, someday...

And then the day came, in this huge room next to his own personal offices, lathered in vintage football memorabilia and photos of old San Francisco.

Thanks to the miracle work of a techie standing behind a console, the big screen is broadcasting the best, most exciting game going on at that time. The others are showing other games.

But that will change. If the Colts are lining up for a punt on the big screen, and the Raiders are lining up for first-and-goal in a tie game with the Broncos, the Raiders game will switch to the big screen with sound.

Down on the floor, watching this Sunday football feast in a plush leather easy chair, is a former player, coach, TV star, bus tour guide, and all-time gamer.

On either side, on any given Sunday, various

friends, family, and first-time guests sit. They'll have eaten omelets and wings.

No commercials allowed.

Just football.

It's work, yes, because every year when members of *Madden NFL*'s development team fly out to talk about next year's edition, he has to know every trend of every team, stay on top of new formations, new stars. Electronic Arts people say that Madden is more involved in the deal than he's ever been.

But, really, this is nothing less than Madden's heaven.

★ ★ ★

When Madden was growing up, his father, the mechanic for the Chevrolet dealership, the guy who had nailed the chicken wire over the windows next to Madden's Lot, said to his son, "Don't start working until you have to. Put off working as long as you can."

Madden smiles, a small smile of satisfaction, because he doesn't like to talk about himself, because he really isn't interested in himself. But how can he *not* smile?

"He said, 'If you can play, play as long as you can play.' And I've played my whole life."

And that's something we can all be thankful for: an ambassador for football unlike any other. An all-star in every way.

And a friend.

AUTHOR'S NOTE ON SOURCES

All the quotes from John Madden in this book are taken from a four-hour interview with Mr. Madden in the lobby of his son's hotel in Pleasanton, California, in 2017. All quotes from former Oakland Raiders players and officials come from two years of personal interviews for my 2011 adult book on the championship Raiders of the 1970s.

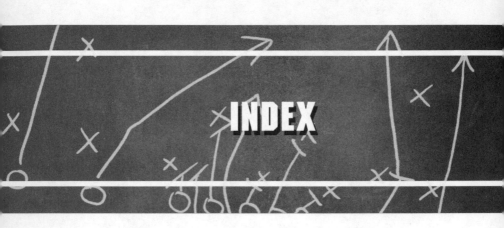

INDEX

INDEX

and John Madden, 48–50,
57–58, 62–67, 93, 112
and Oakland Raiders, 44,
46–48, 52, 56–58, 62–67,
81, 90, 93, 185–186, 189
as young coach, 45, 51
Davis, Clarence, 81–82, 91–92,
106
Denver Broncos, 110, 153

Electronic Arts, 139, 142, 144,
146, 193

Fuqua, Frenchy, 83–85

Governali, Paul, 41–42, 48
Greatest Game Ever Played,
30–31
Green Bay Packers, 22, 31–32,
54, 56, 62, 99
Guy, Ray, 76, 105–106

Hawkins, Trip, 137–144,
146–148
Hendricks, Ted, 71, 94, 106,
184
Hester, Devin, 60, 147
Hunt, Lamar, 52, 54, 138

I formation, 34–35
Immaculate Reception play,
80, 82–85

John Madden Football (video
game), 141, 143

Kansas City Chiefs, 54, 78, 81,
87–88, 138, 185

Lambeau Field, 31
Landry, Tom, 30, 184–185
Lombardi, Vince, 22, 28–33,
45, 54, 56, 62, 109, 113
Lombardi Trophy, 32, 81, 98
Los Angeles Chargers, 25, 51
Los Angeles Rams, 23, 95,
135, 159, 169

Madden, John
and All-Madden Team,
169–174, 188
childhood love of sports,
1–8, 72, 193–194
coaching style of, 68–79
and college sports, 13–18, 27
decision to become a coach,
25–27

197

INDEX

INDEX